GETTING OUT OF DEBT

fastread

GETTING OUT OF DEBT

Repair bad credit and restore your finances!

Rich Mintzer

Adams Media Corporation
Holbrook, Massachusetts

product manager: Gary Krebs
series editor: Michelle Roy Kelly
production director: Susan Beale
production coordinator: Debbie Sidman
layout and graphics: Arlene Apone, Paul Beatrice,
Colleen Cunningham,
Daria Perreault, Frank Rivera

additional research by Donna LaStella

Published by
Adams Media Corporation
260 Center Street, Holbrook, MA 02343, U.S.A.
www.adamsmedia.com

ISBN: 1-58062-509-6

Printed in Canada

J I H G F E D C B A

Library of Congress Cataloging-in-Publication Data available
upon request from the publisher.

This publication is designed to provide accurate and authoritative information
with regard to the subject matter covered. It is sold with the understanding that
the publisher is not engaged in rendering legal, accounting, or other professional
advice. If legal advice or other expert assistance is required, the services of a
competent professional person should be sought.

—From a *Declaration of Principles* jointly adopted by a
Committee of the American Bar Association and a
Committee of Publishers and Associations

This book is available at quantity discounts for bulk purchases.
For information, call 1-800-872-5627.

Visit our exciting home page at www.fastread.com

contents

introduction

Do you spend more money than you earn? Are you tired of living from paycheck to paycheck? Do you make more withdrawals than deposits to your savings account? Are all of your credit cards maxed out?

If you answered yes to one or more of these questions, congratulations, you're most likely in debt. Like the majority of working-class individuals, you seemingly have more expenses than income. Let's face it, in the world today, debt has become an inevitable part of life. You start accruing debt from the time you are born. Just think about how much your parents have invested in you . . . you owe them the biggest payback of all. Student loans, car payments, insurance, and credit cards are necessary evils that everyone encounters at one point or another. Debt forces you to seek more credit and the credit surges you deeper into debt. It truly is a vicious cycle.

But, just because you've entered into debt doesn't mean you have to accept this fate. Many people face financial dilemmas, which at times can be overwhelming, but it doesn't have to go from bad to worse. It is critical for you not to become paralyzed by debt. Instead, take action. A change of lifestyle will be a crucial element to the reversal of your current situation. This book will help show you how to make the most of your money and get out of the cycle of debt. It will also emphasize the importance of staying out of debt and provide guidelines for planning out your future and the future of your family.

Getting out of debt is not an easy process to go through. It just takes a strong commitment, some discipline, and a little will power. By following the steps discussed in this book, you will be well on your way to living debt-free. It won't always be a smooth ride, but the pay-off will make it all worth while. And, with the help of this book, you will learn how to ensure that you don't fall into the debt trap again.

chapter one

Knowing Your Financial Situation

The Importance of Budgets

No matter who you ask or what book or article you may read, the first thing you will learn in order to get out of debt is to create a budget. Having a budget is the single most important step to getting out of debt. A budget will show you exactly where you stand with your finances. Most people have money going out in so many places that it's hard to keep track of how much money is actually being brought home every month, if any at all. Hence the budget will help to better organize you and your spending. Budgets give you the opportunity to see everything in black and white and end some of that frustration you feel when at the end of the month you have no idea where your money has gone. Although creating a budget may seem daunting, it's scarier to go on spending without one.

Budgets are important—there's no doubt about that. If you learn to keep a budget now, it will most certainly help you after you're out of debt. Make it a point to keep using your budget after you are debt free. It will help you put more money into your savings account and toward retirement. It will provide you with a concise and practical vision about what you want to accomplish. It will also help you determine how much you can afford for a new car, new home, or that much-needed vacation.

Many people develop money problems due to a lack of financial planning and/or miscalculating earnings. If you want to change your financial situation you must understand and learn how to manage it first. Sticking to a monthly budget is a good start to managing your money more effectively. Living within specific monetary guidelines doesn't have to be punishment. It can actually be very rewarding. Especially after those nasty debts are paid off and become nothing more than bad memories. You don't have to be a mathematical genius or a bookkeeper to keep one either. The hardest part of a budget is learning how to stay within your means. That's the discipline and willpower part of getting out of debt. It's really not as difficult as it sounds and if you keep a strict record, at the end of the year you will even be able to calculate your net worth.

Just Do It

Creating a budget will take an initial investment of time and focused attention. You will need to determine both your fixed and estimated variable expenses. It could take a couple of months as you track both outgoing and incoming expenses. Take this extra time and scrutinize where you've been spending so that you will be able to decide necessities versus luxuries. Be sure to set specific short-term and long-term goals as well. Would you like to save for a new car? Figure that into your plan. Use the following steps to help you set up your past spending record and future budget.

- **Calculate Your Income:** Income includes your net paycheck (your take-home pay) after withholding taxes and social security. If, however, your primary source of income is derived from freelancing or any other means of self-employment, list your total income then subtract estimated self-employment taxes in your expense column.

  Other sources of income include bonuses, tips, royalties, stock dividends, interest, trust funds, disability benefits, veteran's benefits, alimony, child support, and even gifts and gambling winnings. Any definite income source should be included. This is for your eyes only, so be honest. When you are through listing your sources of income, combine the total.

- **Determine the Essential Expenses:** The essentials are those bills that have to be paid regularly. *Fixed expenses* are those that remain the same from month to month. These include rent or mortgage payments, insurance, auto loans, and student loans. It is usually difficult to move these expenses into a lower, more comfortable amount, but it can be done. *Variable expenses* have *varying* amounts from month to month. Be sure to include groceries, utilities, telephone, healthcare, retirement, and putting gas in the car. Don't forget the little extras like haircuts, toiletries, and parking tolls as well as savings for both short- and long-term goals. Be sure to check over your list weekly, when first starting out, to find those hidden expenses that can be easily overlooked.

- **Determine the Nonessential Expenses:** Book and magazine subscriptions, restaurant bills, entertainment (going to the movies, playing miniature golf, having a drink with friends), vacations, new clothes, birthday presents, and assorted gifts all fall under this category.
- **Make a Weekly List:** A weekly list will help keep your spending record in check. It can be a real eye-opener when you start to see what you've really been spending on. If you are not sure about how much you have spent, just estimate. If you think you spend $10 a week on coffee, round that to $15. It's better to budget for more and have money left over than to come up short.
- **Devise a Monthly Budget:** Following is a chart that can be used or changed to best suit your needs. The months are left blank so that you can start the chart at any point in the year. Keep in mind, that in order to make your budget work, you need to know when you have reached your spending limit in a particular category. Thus the reason for the weekly spending list. When you've reached the limit, it's time to unleash the will power and stop spending in that category.

Keep in mind that a well-structured budget should:

1. Be easy to follow.
2. Fit into your lifestyle.
3. Cover all expenses and sources of income.
4. Leave room for expansion.
5. Suit your individual or family needs.
6. Help you meet your financial goals.

MONTHLY BUDGET CHART

FIXED EXPENSES:	MONTHLY PAYMENT	CHECK IF TAX DEDUCTIBLE
Mortgage/Rent		
Insurance (auto/home/medical)		
Auto Payments		
Personal/Student Loans		
Savings/Holiday Accounts*		
TOTAL FIXED EXPENSES		

VARIABLE EXPENSES:	MONTHLY PAYMENT	CHECK IF AMOUNT IS DECREASING
Utilities (gas/electric/water)		
Food		
Credit Cards		
Household expenses		
Personal Hygiene		
Laundry/Dry Cleaning		
Clothing**		
Entertainment		
Gifts/Miscellaneous		
TOTAL VARIABLE EXPENSES		

* There is a monthly payment slot for a savings account. Even if it is just $5 a week until you are out of debt, a savings account should be a part of your fixed expenses.

** This is something that does not have to be a monthly expense but rather a reward to yourself when you have met your goals.

Sample Budget

INCOME	ANNUAL	MONTHLY
His annual income (net pay)	$37,500	$3,125
Her annual income (net pay)	$37,500	$3,125
Stocks/savings, dividends, and interest (estimate)	$3,000	$250
Investment, capital gains	$2,400	$200
TOTAL	$80,000	$6,700

EXPENSES		
Rent/Mortgage (including insurance)	$18,000	$1,500
Insurance	$3,000	$250
Medical	$5,000	$415
Travel/Vacation	$2,500	$210
Food and daily items	$15,000	$1,250
Clothing	$6,000	$500
Entertainment	$6,000	$250
Utilities and telephone	$4,000	$335
Auto	$5,500	$460
Home Related	$3,000	$250
Gifts	$500	$40
Charitable contributions	$500	$40
Miscellaneous	$1,500	$125
Child Care	$5,000	$415
School	$500	$40
Savings	$3,000	$250
TOTAL	$79,000	$6,330

AVAILABLE CASH	$1,000*

* Although it seems that there is $1,000 left over as disposable income, this is not the case if you are in debt. This money is likely spent on numerous small incidentals. Perhaps you drove to a party at your in-laws (5 hours away) and spent some additional money on fuel and snacks for the drive. Or maybe someone in your office was selling Girl Scout cookies and, feeling generous, you bought four boxes. Who knows? The point is the money seems to be going out at a rate that is much faster than it is coming in. That's the issue here. You need to uncover and account for all hidden expenses.

Once your budget is set you can begin to look for ways to cut back on expenses and spending. The following list offers some suggestions.

1. Buy no-frills or generic brands at the grocery store whenever you can.
2. Use coupons as often as possible. You'll be surprised how much they add up.
3. Instead of throwing away returnable cans and bottles, return them and put the extra cash towards your groceries. While it's only a small amount, combined with coupons and no-frill shopping it could very well put a large dent in your monthly grocery bill.
4. Consider changing your phone company. Most people don't realize how much they spend on one phone call; many people just look at how much they owe and then pay that amount.
5. Put a timer and a log next to your telephone. Keep track of how long you are on the phone and how many phone calls you make a day. Make a conscious effort to cut back.
6. Bring your lunch to work as often as possible.
7. Get a movie from the library instead of renting one or going out to the movies.
8. Figure out what your daily miscellaneous expenses are and give yourself a smaller portion of that as a weekly allowance. The first couple of weeks you will probably spend it in a couple of days. Don't break down and give yourself more money. Figure a way to live without that spare cash until you give yourself the next week's allowance and try to make that last a week.

9. Turn your heat down at night in the winter and run your air conditioner less in the summer.

10. Turn off the lights when you're not in the room. Switch to a lower wattage bulb to bring the utility bills down.

11. Don't leave lights on when you are going out, and curb other means of electricity.

12. Avoid late charges at all costs. Pay your bills as soon as they come in the mail. It's better not to send bills too close to the due date. They may get lost in the mail and you will now have late penalty fees to pay as well; as if the interest you are paying isn't enough.

13. Visit a price club like BJ's or Costco on occasion and stock up on foods and supplies that will last. This is particularly helpful if you have a large family.

14. Don't always spend money on goods or services that you can make or do for yourself. For example, you can occasionally cut your child's hair or make a greeting card yourself.

15. Don't buy three when one will do. This goes for ordering premium cable TV channels, magazine subscriptions, sneakers, and so on.

16. Consider buying a used car instead of a new one. (More information is provided in a later section).

17. Take care of what you own. From changing the oil in your car to keeping the heads clean on your VCR, the better you maintain what you have, the less often you will have to replace things.

18. Don't be suckered in by every new technological time saver. Universal remotes, automatic phone dialers, and other gimmicks have proven to be completely unnecessary. This also includes upgrading

your computer software every time a highly pro-
moted newer model comes out.

19. Throw spare change into a jar. When you have
filled the jar celebrate with a "Spare Change Night."
Those nickels, dimes, and quarters can really add up
and you won't be tapping into your budget at all.

20. Look for discounts and sales on clothing and appli-
ances. Avoid impulse buying and shop around for
the best bargains and prices.

Budgets For Different Times in Life

A budget for a twenty-four-year old and for a sixty-four-year old
will include a lot of the same items; however, the priorities placed
on those items and the money allotted will change significantly
over that forty year span. For example, at twenty-four an automobile is really just a mode of transportation, usually for one. It will
not be a vehicle that needs to last many years and can often be a
used car. At thirty-four, a car may need to accommodate the entire
family and will therefore need to be larger and more durable. A
second car may be necessary as well. At sixty-four, you may want
a lot of room for grandchildren or have saved up enough to get the
car you always dreamed of. Or, you might decide that since you
are living in a retirement community and rarely have the need to
travel, you can lease a car. The point is that the expenses will vary.

Another example might be the money a single person
spends on weekly dances or trips to trendy clubs versus the
money a married couple spends on a baby-sitter for their children. (Different idea but the same line item.) The single
person spends $100 for the evening out, including a new shirt;
the married couple spends $25 on the sitter and $75 for dinner
and a movie.

Budgeting for Milestones

Planning for weddings and other major events means you will need to adjust your budget for a specific period of time. Unlike saving to pay for college tuition or putting aside money for retirement, these are significant events that will cost a significant amount of money at one time. While a wedding need not cost as much as a year of college, it can cost more, depending on the size and scope of the occasion.

The idea for preparing for any major potential expense (be it buying a car or planning a trip to Europe) is to set up a savings plan with enough advance time to allow your money to work for you. Also allow for inflation, as costs will be higher for a wedding in five years than they are now. Often, saving for a special event, such as a vacation, is a strong incentive to put money aside regularly.

Budgeting for Vacations

Factoring in at the start of the year how much you think you can set aside for your vacation will help you determine where you can afford to go. If you have a particular destination in mind, check out the airfare and cost per day with a travel agent or through guidebooks to that destination of choice. The best travel season for most people is the summer. However, if you can travel at a non-peak time of year, you can usually spend less. As for your budget, you should start setting aside money at the start of the year.

If you are planning to travel in August, you are looking at budgeting your trip through seven months. Therefore, if the vacation will cost $2,500 for two people, you need to put aside $357 per month for each of those seven months leading to the trip. If you have a lump sum coming in, you could simply put it in a short-term low-risk account for six months and gain some interest on it.

Budgeting for the trip, however, may mean that you should move another major purchase to the fall, when the vacation line on your budget can be replaced with payments for another item.

Need Help?

If you are having a difficult time putting a budget together, consider asking a friend you trust to assist you. If that doesn't work out, look into a reputable budget planner. While it will cost you money, it might be worth the expense to spare the aggravation of doing it yourself. Some places will even get you set on a budget for free, but in general the cost is under $100. If you feel that you may need more help than just budget preparations, a debt counselor may suit your needs best. (More information to follow.)

chapter two

Finding Alternative Sources of Income

You may find that you simply do not have enough income to adequately cover your expenses. If this is the case, it may be in your best interest to seek out alternative sources of income.

The Part-Time Job

The most obvious additional source of income is a second job. A second job will not only help increase your cash flow, but to a small advantage, it will keep you so busy you won't have time to frivolously spend money!

The most important thing to consider when taking a second job is its overall worth. Make sure that the positives of the job outweigh the negatives. You wouldn't want to spend more money on gas or bus fare than you would actually be earning. If you have children, consider the extra daycare or baby-sitting costs you may incur.

Be sure to decide ahead of time how you will use the money from this job. You may want to put it all towards paying bills, deposit it directly into your savings account, or use it as your weekly spending money (depending on how much you earn).

Consider These Part-Time Jobs
Newspaper delivery
Baby-sitting
Telemarketing
Small appliance repair
Dog walking
Pet sitting
House cleaning
Companion to the elderly
Stuffing envelopes
Store clerk
Word processing
Freelance writing

Rental Income

If you own a home, consider renting out a room or apartment to someone. Be sure to check the local zoning regulations and guidelines before doing so. Also, think long and hard about whether you want to take on such an added responsibility. Although the income may be nice, the headaches that go along with being a landlord may outweigh the money.

Out With the Old, In With the Cash

Clean out your garage or attic and have a yard sale. Sometimes feeling like you're getting a fresh start helps put things in perspective. The money you make on the sale could be a starting point for a savings account or enough to make a dent in paying off one of those terrible credit card balances.

Refinancing Mortgages vs. Home Equity Loans

If you own property, there are two very useful options you have that can be powerful tools when getting out of debt. The first is refinancing your mortgage. Most people refinance a mortgage to get a lower interest rate, which in turn will produce a lower monthly payment. (More information on this subject can be found in the section on home buying). Refinancing is only beneficial if it will save you 2 percentage points or more. When you refinance your mortgage, there are closing costs involved so you will need to factor that into your calculations.

While refinancing a home saves money on monthly payments there is a second option available to some homeowners. A home equity loan is like a mortgage except that you are borrowing money against a percentage of the equity you have in your home. Most people take out home equity loans to do remodeling, add additions or to pay off their existing debts. Home equity loans are generally a minimum of 5 percentage points less than credit card rates. Another bonus to the home equity loan is that it is tax deductible and there are no closing costs attached.

Here's the bad news: If you default on your mortgage or home equity loan, you could stand a chance of losing your home. Lenders are not as lenient with home loans as they are with credit card loans. If you decide to apply for a home equity loan, generally you will need to have been paying on your mortgage for at least one year. Another important point to remember is that home equity loans are given out to improve on your home; that is when your interest payments are tax deductible. If you pay off your credit cards with your home equity loan, be sure to save all receipts for any work you do on your home any time thereafter. If you have strictly used this money for your debt and then try to get a tax deduction, Uncle Sam will not be very happy about this. You will get penalized.

Some food for thought: If you have a $100,000, 30-year mortgage, include $50 extra with each monthly payment. You will not only pay off the loan six years ahead of time, but you will also save $40,000 in interest.

chapter three

Credit Cards

Credit cards are a wonderful invention. They can help us when an emergency comes along, and they allow us to make a purchase before the money is even in the bank. From department stores to gas stations to the local food emporium, every retail outlet, catalog, home shopping network, and Internet site will offer you the chance to pay by credit card. They make shopping from home via computer or television very easy. They are the technological IOUs that allow for tremendously increased purchasing power. If used wisely, credit cards can reward you with freebies like frequent flier miles or discounts on just about anything. If used incorrectly, they can also cause a great deal of damage.

It is estimated that Americans now charge over $600 billion on credit cards each year. So, how does one control the urge to whip out that plastic card and walk away with goods and/or services? Personality has a lot to do with it.

First, there are individuals for whom credit cards are a convenient way to avoid carrying around a wad of cash. These people pay their monthly bills in full and on time. They are aware of how much they can charge at any given point in time and are always able to pay in full. Essentially, they manage their money well and use credit cards to supplement their income.

However, too many individuals end up spending money they don't have. Spend now, pay later is the basic premise here. Consumers need to stop thinking of their credit limits as money they can freely use and stop spending as a way to cope with stress. Buying something to make yourself feel better may seem like a good idea at the time, but this pattern of spending will have serious consequences later on. The individual who, by his or her nature, seeks instant gratification is more likely to run into credit card debt than the person who plans ahead.

The credit card industry is hoping that their tantalizing sales approach, led by commercial television, tempts you to just go out and buy. Apparently the temptation is great, as the credit card industry is booming. Beware. Purchasing power can be dangerous!

Break the Cycle of Credit Debt

The consequences of credit card debt can be scary, but they can also be overcome. Here are some basic guidelines to reducing credit card debt:

- Stop charging! In fact, don't even carry the cards in your wallet or purse. If the card is accessible, chances are you will use it.

- Always pay more than the minimum balance and disregard so-called "Payment Holidays." In this way, you will pay more than just the monthly interest accrued. You should begin to see a significant decrease in the balance within a few months.

- If you have two or more credit cards, consolidate the debt. Use the card with the lowest interest rate to pay off the other cards. Checks are sent every month with your statement that can be used for this purpose. Now you will have only one bill to worry about each month and you will be accruing less interest. Another idea is to make larger payments to the card with a higher interest rate and balance while making minimum payments on the other card(s). As soon as one is paid off start making larger payments to the card with the next highest balance.

- Ask to have your interest rate reduced. Most banks will do this if they see that you have made your payments on time and have been a consistent or long-term customer. If your bank refuses, then you may want to start shopping around for a new card. In checking out new possibilities pay close attention to the fine print. Make sure that the interest rate being offered will remain the same for balance transfers and that there are no extra fees charged. You can check online to see what rates lenders are currently offering at (*www.bankrate.com*). If you sign up for a card with a low interest rate that suddenly skyrockets, hop to another card. Transferring a balance can be a smart move, but only if you get a lower interest rate and have a plan to pay off the balance quickly. At the risk of sounding cliché again, you have to learn when to say yes and when to say no.

The Dreaded Interest

Besides avoiding cards that have high interest rates, you should also find out how the interest is calculated by each individual bank. Avoid cards with a "two-cycle average daily balance method." In a two-cycle plan, the average daily balance is based on two month's spending instead of one. If you don't see this information anywhere on your statement, call the lender and check it out. Although not an issue with all credit cards, look out for annual fees. If the annual fee is high, you might not see the advantage in a lower interest rate.

Banks rely on the fact that the average consumer is not going to calculate the actual amount of interest they are paying. Savvy card holders who try to close their accounts tend to get sucked back in by the promise of larger lines of credit or reduced minimum payments. This alone is reason to pay off your cards every month.

Credit Card Blocking

You may not have heard of credit card blocking, but inevitably, you've probably fallen prey to it without knowing. Basically, credit blocking is preauthorization to charge an amount to your credit card for services to be provided. This most often happens when you book a hotel room or rent a car in advance.

When you call to make the booking, the hotel or rental agent in turn notifies the creditor electronically of your request. Then a hold is placed on your card for the specified amount and it is deducted from your credit limit at that time. Blocks typically last between ten and fifteen days; but they may last longer.

The major problem that can result from credit card blocking is that you may be over your limit without even realizing it. This will become an issue if you are already carrying a balance that is very close to your credit limit.

If you pay the bill with the same credit card you used for booking, the block should be removed within a few days. If you decide to pay the bill in cash or with a different credit card, the block will most likely remain for the full fifteen days or more. Even though you paid the bill, the first card company has no knowledge of the transaction.

Secured Cards

With secured credit cards you put up a deposit in advance, usually somewhere between $500 and $3,000. This then becomes your line of credit, so you are essentially borrowing against yourself. The reason for doing this is to make sure you pay your charges every month (there's usually an annual fee). Secured credit cards are good for building up a credit rating (showing you can pay on time). If you want to acquire other credit cards, apply for a loan, or get a mortgage, a secured card is a good starting point.

Building a good line of credit (or restoring a history of bad credit) where the issuer increases the amount you can charge, will occur as you use the card and pay your monthly bills on time. A good line of credit will make you a "good credit risk" which is important if you will apply for a mortgage or another type of loan in the future.

Many consumers are unaware that some of the secured card issuers do not report to the credit bureaus. If you intend to apply for one of these cards, be sure to ask if your history and information will be reported. If the issuer doesn't report your use of the card, trying to establish good credit with it will be null and void. There are also extra fees in some cases to obtain a secured card and they typically carry higher interest rates.

Keep One in Your Maiden Name

Women who share cards with their husbands often neglect to double check that they have their own individual credit rating. Credit card companies may not even list you jointly. Should you get divorced or should your husband die, you then have no credit rating. Request at least one credit card in your legal name, even on joint accounts.

Students and Credit

The Consumer Federation of America (*www.consumerfed.org*) recently posted a study about college students and credit. The study indicates that previous research had underestimated the extent of college students' debt and related problems (including suicides of indebted students). Marketing efforts on behalf of creditors can be aggressive, seductive, and effective in getting more and more vulnerable college students to apply for credit. About 70 percent of undergraduates at four year colleges have in their possession at least one credit card, carrying thousands of dollars in debt.

Students from affluent families who build up sizable debt are typically bailed out by their parents. Unfortunately, students who come from families with modest incomes are typically asked to cut back on their course work and take on part-time jobs to pay off their debts. In the worst case scenarios, students are forced to drop out of school and work full-time. Some schools have reported losing more students to credit card debt than to academic failure.

Additionally, when students start looking for employment, they are finding it difficult to get work because employers are reviewing their credit reports.

Financial stress can have a psychological impact as well. Problems can range from anxiety to emotional crisis resulting in suicide. Students fall into debt through the extension of unaffordable credit lines, increasing education-related expenses, peer pressure to spend, and financial naiveté reinforced by low minimum payments.

While the government is working on the problem of restricting creditors, and universities are doing the same in the case of college students, there is good reason for parents to get involved with their teenage children as well. On top of their credit debt, when they finish school some students have a student loan to pay back as well. The financial dilemma can be overwhelming. While there are some good tips anyone can tell a college student in a book, inevitably they will still need to see the results of their actions. Prevention is truly the best solution to the problem of students and the dangers of credit card debt. Teaching kids early on about the value of money is the key to keeping them from making the same mistakes millions of Americans make every day. (For more information see the section entitled, *Teach Your Children Well*).

chapter four

Credit Reports and You

A consumer credit report is a factual record of an individual's credit payment history. It is provided for a purpose permitted by law, primarily to credit grantors. Its main purpose is to help a lender quickly and objectively decide whether to grant you credit. There are three major companies handling credit ratings in the United States: Equifax, Experian Information Solutions, and Trans Union. These credit bureaus are not in the business of issuing or denying credit cards. They establish your credit reports from the reports given to them. You have a right, by law to see your credit report.

If you have any of the following, you probably have information stored in one or all of the consumer credit databases: a credit card, car loan, student loan, or home mortgage. Most of the information in your credit report comes directly from the companies you do business with, but some information comes from public records.

Credit reports do not include any information on bank accounts; medical history; large purchases paid by cash or check; your race, gender, religion, or nationality. The typical credit report does contain four types of information: **identifying information, credit information, public record information,** and **inquiry information.** Identifying information includes the basics: name, address, Social Security number, year of birth, and current/previous employers. This information is compiled from any and all credit applications you fill out. The credit information that is contained in your report is specific data about each account (date opened, credit limit, loan balance, payment patterns, etc.) Public record information is exactly that: federal district bankruptcy records, court records, tax liens, and monetary judgments. The inquiry information section comprises a list of the persons or companies who have requested a copy of your credit report for any reason.

Maintaining a good credit report is equally important. The ability to have and retain a good credit rating allows consumers many benefits including low interest rates, housing, and employment.

Checking and reviewing your report is also important. You want to ensure that the data on your report is correct. Negative data can lessen your chances of obtaining credit, renting an apartment, or even getting a new job. Many law firms and banks will review a possible candidate's credit along with their employment history.

It's a good idea to check your credit report once a year. In most cases, you can obtain a report free of charge from any of the bureaus once a year (see Appendix A). Some states do charge a small fee. Another reason to check your report is to make sure there are no fraudulent charges or credit cards listed that you don't know about. The final reason to check your report is to make sure that anyone out there with the same name doesn't get his/her credit mixed up with yours. Juniors and seniors need to be particularly mindful of the latter.

The amount of time information stays on your report differs depending on the type of information. To prevent past errors from haunting you forever, federal law deems the length of stay for specific information. Most negative information must be taken off after a period of seven years. Bankruptcy information remains for a longer period of time. All positive data remains for the duration of the report.

The federal Fair Credit Reporting Act (FCRA) protects consumers who apply for credit and are then denied. If you have been denied credit based on information in your credit report, the credit lender is required by law to tell you the name and address of the credit bureau used to acquire the information. Along the same line, the credit bureau must supply free of charge a copy of your report, but only if you request it from them within a sixty-day period of your denial.

How to Obtain Your Credit Report

The credit reporting agencies provide three ways to obtain a copy of your report. Consumers can request a report by logging on to an agency's Web site, writing the agency, or calling the agency directly.

Equifax
P.O. Box 105496
Atlanta GA 30348-5496
800/997-2493
www.equifax.com

Experian
P.O. Box 2014
Allen TX 75013
888/EXPERIAN
www.experian.com

Trans Union
P.O. Box 1000
Chester PA 19022
800/888-4213
www.transunion.com

Reading and Understanding Your Credit Report

Please refer to sample credit reports in Appendix A.

When you receive your credit report, a guide should accompany it. It might be printed on the back of the report. The guide will explain how to read the report and help to decipher the numbers and codes used. Each credit bureau has its own format. When you receive the report, check to make sure the personal information is correct. Look closely at the spelling of your name, your address, date of birth, and your social security number.

- **Public Record Information:** If you have ever filed for bankruptcy or had a lien or judgment filed against you it will be listed in this section. The information contained in regard to these matters would be the type of bankruptcy (Chapter 7 or 13), date filed and amounts of liabilities, assets and exemptions. If you have filed a judgment against another party, this will also be on the report.

Remember to check the dates in this section; most items can only be listed for seven years.

- **Collections Information:** Sometimes collections are listed in the Account Information Section. If it is not related to a credit account it will appear separately. Mainly medical and insurance collections will be listed here. The information in this section will include: the collection agency involved, the company that is owed money, the amount owed and date when it was reported, and any activity since reporting it.

- **Credit Account Information:** Lists all of your credit cards, department store cards, mortgages, auto loans, and other bank loans. Specifics include account numbers, the date the account was opened, the date of last activity, credit limit, terms of the account, current balance, and past due amounts.

- **Additional Information:** This section is used for foreclosures and checking accounts. Checking account information is only included if the account was closed for insufficient funds.

- **Inquiries Section:** This comes in two parts. The first part is a listing of any company you authorized to obtain a copy of your report. Anyone making an inquiry will see this section. The second part contains inquiries that are not reported to businesses. This part of the report is for your eyes only. It consists of inquiries where your name and address were given to creditors so that they could offer you an application for credit. Another type of inquiry that would show up would be those made by your existing creditor. If your credit card is with Bank of America, they will periodically check your credit report to see how your credit history is progressing. This section will also show if you have ever requested a copy for yourself.

- **Risk Scores:** On some credit reports a risk score is shown. The main purpose of a risk score is to aid creditors in their decision-making process of approving or denying an application. The process of risk scoring is a statistical summary of all the information provided on your report. The score determines how likely you are to repay your debts. Numerical values are assigned to specific pieces of data on your report. These values are then put through a series of mathematical calculations that in turn produce a single number. This number becomes your risk score.

You are ultimately in control of your risk score. Work toward paying your bills on time, keeping credit card balances low, and checking your credit report periodically for inaccuracies.

Fixing Errors

There are two very important reasons to dispute inaccuracies on your credit report. Foremost is that when you apply for credit or a loan, you could be denied due to discrepancies between the application you fill out and the actual credit report. Secondly, you may be held responsible for someone else's debt. Your report may list fraudulent accounts set up by someone who "borrowed" your identity.

Thousands of Americans are unaware that another person may be using their personal information to get car loans and credit cards. These individuals then default on the payments, leaving you, the unassuming victim to pick up the pieces. If there are any errors, you should contact the credit bureau immediately and have an investigation started.

All reports come with a phone number and address to contact the agency. Some even include a dispute form. All you need do is fill it out and send it back to the company.

Reporting Credit Repair Scams

Credit repair companies are expensive and often entice consumers who have histories of bad credit. If you have negative credit data on your report it will be removed after seven years (10 years for bankruptcy). If you seek out the assistance of a credit repair service, make note that they can not charge you until six months after the services have been rendered. The law also requires these companies to provide consumers with a written contract that clearly states all of the services it will provide for you and the terms of payment. Under this law, you have three days to withdraw from the contract if you choose to do so. This law helps to protect the consumer from fraudulent businesses.

If you do decide to use the services of a credit repair agency, beware of scams. Don't be seduced by slogans like "No Credit? No Problem!" or "We Erase Bad Credit—100% Guaranteed!" The truth is that no one can deliver on those types of promises. *No one can legally remove negative credit information from your report.*

Keep in mind that anything a credit repair service does, you can do. If you've found errors on your report, contact the credit bureau directly. Do the research yourself and get to the bottom of the issue before it is too late.

chapter five

Collection Agencies

Worse than dealing with the debt itself is the prospect of dealing with collection agencies. Although it is an uncomfortable situation to be in, it is best to try to stay calm and in control when dealing with these individuals. Understanding how these agents work and devising a plan of payment will help to make the situation easier.

Creditors (the bank, store, etc. that issued your credit) sometimes have departments within their own companies that handle unpaid accounts. If you fail to pay a bill and it becomes overdue (usually sixty days or more), the bill defaults to the collection department. It is the collection department's job to get the money from you. If the amount you owe is not significant, the company might decide to make the amount owed a "charge-off." Charge-offs are funds lost by a credit lender. If a lender decides to charge-off your amount due, it will appear as such on your credit report. However, the company may decide to turn the matter over to a collection agency. Each company is different. Some lenders might refer your claim to the collection department as soon as thirty days have passed. Others will wait sixty days.

Your best strategy in avoiding a confrontation with the credit agency is to make contact with your creditor as soon as you realize you will not be able to pay your debt. If you don't make the first move, it is likely to send the message that you have no intention of paying. If you know in advance that you will not be able to pay a bill, call the creditor and try to work out a payment plan that will work for both sides. Creditors are usually not prepared for this approach and you may see better results because you took the first step and caught them off guard. By doing so, you may avoid having to deal with collection agencies at all. In preparation, have a clear objective about what you want to accomplish. For example, if you owe a creditor $100 payments each month; negotiate and try to get the payments lowered to $75 a month, or whatever amount you can more easily afford. Once you arrange for a new repayment plan, make sure you stick to the terms. Otherwise, you will most surely be contacted by a collection agency.

If you have already started getting calls from collectors, keep your cool. Be sure to keep a record of all the calls you receive and include the name of the person you spoke with. DO NOT TAPE THE CALLS. This practice is against the law and can only get you in deeper trouble. Write the important information down and keep it close to the phone for easy access. The information in your log will be important in future conversations with the company.

Try to avoid fueling the fire of antagonism in the phone call. If the collector becomes rude or harasses you in any way, you have a right to take legal action against them. Do not be afraid to let them know that you are aware of their harassment and that you will not stand for it. Your mantra should be, "Unfortunately, I will be unable to pay back that amount by XX date. However, I would like to set up an alternative payment plan that will be beneficial to both of us." If that doesn't work, just remember that the law is on your side.

The Federal Government looks out for our better interests when it comes to collection agencies. As such, the Fair Debt Collection Practices Act (FDCPA), outlined below, was passed in 1977. The FDCPA outlaws unfair and ruthless practices used by debt collectors. Personal, family, and household debts are all covered by the Act. Unfortunately, some collectors fail to follow this law. Sadly, the law is broken most often when debt collectors are dealing with persons whose primary language is not English.

An Outline of the Fair Debt Collection Practices Act (FDCPA)

- You may stop a collector from contacting you by writing them return receipt mail, and telling them to stop. Once the agency receives your letter, they may only contact you to say there will be no further contact. The agency may also notify you if the debt collector or the creditor intends to take some specific action against you such as a law suit. **Reminder:** Writing to the collector does not make the debt go away. You still owe the money and you could still be sued by the creditor or the collection agency.
- A collector may contact you in person, by mail, phone, fax, or telegram.
- If you have an attorney, the collector must contact the attorney rather than you personally.

- Collection agencies may **NOT** contact you before 8:00 A.M. and after 9:00 P.M.

- Collection agencies may **NOT** contact you at unreasonable places such as hospitals or rehabilitation facilities unless you agree.

- Collection agencies may **NOT** contact you at work if you have specifically told them that your employer does not approve of the contact.

- Within five days after you are first contacted, the debt collector must send you a written notice of the debt owed; how much and to whom; and what action you should take if you feel there has been an error.

- Collection agencies are **NOT** to misrepresent themselves as agents of the government, attorneys, or as employees of credit bureaus. They can't use false names either, although many do.

- Collection agencies are **NOT** allowed to make false statements. For example they can't imply that you have committed a crime (since you have not). They can't say that you'll go to jail, they can't lie about the status of legal documents they are sending you, and they can't say they'll garnish or withhold your wages.

- Collection agencies may **NOT** contact other people about you except to find out where you live or work. They cannot reveal how much debt you owe to other people or publish a list of people who have bad debt. In other words, they cannot slander your reputation.

- Collection agencies may **NOT** verbally abuse you, threaten your life, or use profanity. (Once again, many do.)

- Collection agencies may **NOT** cause your telephone to ring and ring, or engage any person in telephone conversation repeatedly or continuously with intent to annoy, abuse, or harass any person at the called number.

If a debt collection has proven to be in violation of your rights, it is in your best interest to take action. Report violations from a debt collector to your state Attorney General's office and the Federal Trade Commission. Many states have their own debt collection laws and your Attorney General's office can help you determine your rights. There are three ways you can contact the Federal Trade Commission's Consumer Response Center:

> *Phone:* toll-free 877/FTC-HELP (382-4357)
> *Regular mail:*
> Federal Trade Commission
>   CRC-240
>   600 Pennsylvania Avenue NW
>   Washington, D.C. 20580
> *Electronically:* Fill out the complaint form at
> *(www.ftc.gov/ftc/complaint.htm).*

Send a copy of the complaint and a letter to your state's consumer protection agency as well as the creditor who hired the collection agency. If the violations are severe enough, the creditor may very well cease the collection process.

However, if you choose to ignore a collection agency's attempts to contact you, a law suit can be filed against you. If the situation gets to this stage the consequences of your debt will multiply. Once a collector sues you, they can become more aggressive with their actions. A collector can garnish your wages for up to 25 percent of your net income. That's after Uncle Sam takes his share. A collector might also try to seize any money you have in the bank; they may even try to place a lien on your property. If you don't own any property or if you are unemployed, a court order can be placed against you that could last up to twenty years. You really don't want to find yourself in this type of a situation.

Debt Consolidation

Beware that there are many debt consolidation scams running rampant online and on television. If you are considering debt consolidation as an option, it is in your best interest to talk to a credit counselor. Many of these organization are nonprofit and charge a small fee (usually $60 or less) to help you set up a repayment plan. Each month you deposit money with the credit counseling agency; they in turn pay your creditors.

A successful repayment plan will require that you make full, timely payments each month. It could take up to two years to complete. Remember, a debt repayment plan will not erase your previous credit history. In fact, the repayment plan itself will show up on your credit report. However, a demonstrated pattern of timely payments will help you to get credit in the future.

Where to Go

You will want to be sure that the agency you choose will be the best for you. Don't be afraid to interview several potential agencies and ask lots of questions. Any reputable credit agency should also be ready, willing, and able to send you free information about their services through the mail.

The Federal Trade Commission recommends asking the following questions when choosing an agency:

- What specific services are offered?
- Can they help you not only with your present situation, but also work with you to develop a plan of staying debt-free in the future?

- Is there a fee for services? How much and how often? Do you have to pay prior to receiving services?
- Will a formal written contract be drawn up?
- How soon could the agency begin working with you?
- Who regulates or supervises the agency?
- What type of credentials do the counselors have? How many counselors will you be dealing with?
- Will the information be kept confidential?
- How high must your debt be to qualify for services?
- How do you determine the amount of repayment?
- How does the repayment plan work? How will you know if the creditors have received payment?
- Will status reports of your account be made available to you?
- Can the agency get creditors to lower or eliminate interest and finance charges or waive late fees?
- Is a debt repayment plan the only option for you?
- What happens if you can't maintain the agreed-upon plan?
- What debts will be excluded from the plan? Will the agency help plan for the payment of these debts?
- How secure is the information you are providing to the agency?

Here are the names of some agencies you may want to contact.

American Credit Counselors Corporation
(www.billfree.org)
16507 Northcross Drive, Suite F
Huntersville, NC, 28708
888/BILL-FREE
E-mail: *info@billfree.com*

Community Credit Counselors
(www.debt911.org)
3540 Austin Bluffs Parkway, Suite L-1
Colorado Springs, CO, 80918
E-mail: *debt_buster@ibm.net*

Myvesta.org
(www.myvesta.org)
Suite 200, 6 Taft Court
Rockville, MD, 20850
800/680-3328
E-mail: *info@myvesta.org*
One of the nation's first nonprofit, Internet-based financial service companies. The organization is committed to helping people resolve past financial mistakes, manage current financial responsibilities, and find financial peace of mind. Programs and services include debt management, crisis resolution, online bill management, creditor problem resolution, and counseling.

National Foundation for Credit Counseling
(www.nfcc.org)
8611 Second Avenue, Suite 100
Silver Spring MD, 20910
301/589-5600
E-mail: *questions@nfcc.org*
A nonprofit network of over 1,400 "Financial Care Centers" that help people with all types of financial problems through counseling and education.

chapter six

Personal Bankruptcy: The Final Option

A last resort, should you find yourself in tremendous debt, is to file for personal bankruptcy. This is a legal procedure which serves to help people who are in debt start over. It is not an easy decision for people to make, but sometimes it is necessary. Filing for bankruptcy is best advised when your debt has exceeded your annual income and is growing at a faster rate than your potential future income. It is also recommended when you are being sued by creditors. The decision to file for personal bankruptcy is one that must be well thought out and handled carefully by a good bankruptcy attorney, not someone advertising that they can solve all your problems in a hurry. In fact, a good bankruptcy attorney will be the one who first looks to find other alternatives. One of the problems today is that too many people jump the gun and file at the recommendation of an over-anxious attorney.

The Three Forms of Bankruptcy

Should you reach the decision that your only alternative is to file for bankruptcy, there are three options: You can file under Chapter 7, 11, or 13. Individuals generally file under a Chapter 7 or 13, while businesses primarily file under Chapter 11.

Filing under Chapter 7 or "straight bankruptcy" involves liquidating your assets. You turn over the bulk of your assets (those that are not exempt by state or federal law) to the court, which in turn sells them off to pay your creditors. All your debt is discharged, and you do not use your future income to repay any remaining debt. Each state has its own laws regarding exemptions or assets that can not be sold off by the courts. Some states allow you to retain your house, but most include at least a portion of it as equity.

Personal bankruptcy is not pleasant. However, on a positive note, you are out of debt and free to start over again. All transactions are frozen in time when the papers are signed. Therefore, the creditors can not come after you with a lawsuit. No more interest can be added, and nothing should be done by either party—the courts are in control at this point.

You should not try to hide assets by moving them into another area. It is not wise to try to fool the courts by hiding assets; fraud carries stiff penalties. Also, once you have entered into an agreement with a lender, of any kind, from that agreement on, almost any of the money you've moved is fair game for your creditors. In other words, if you buy a home and then start sending $500 a month to a friend, the banks, if you ever declare bankruptcy, can go after the $500 monthly amount you sent to your friend, from the date the lending agreement was signed.

A Chapter 13 ("reorganization") or 11 filing both include the taking of future disposable income and giving it to a trustee of the bankruptcy system who distributes the money to your creditors. The trustee then pays off your bills based on a payment schedule set up with your creditors. Depending on state laws, you often pay off less than the full amount on the dollar. For example, based on your income, you might be expected to pay only $30,000, over five years, of a $50,000 debt. The rest would then be dismissed. Creditors have to agree to the plan, and you can take up to five years (the average time is three years) to pay off the agreed-upon portion of the debt. You need to look at the earning capability of any disposable income, then you need to look at the asset base. This is feasible for someone who has fallen into debt but now has enough steady income to pay it back.

A Chapter 11 filing, designed primarily as a form of business bankruptcy, also allows you to maintain possession of your assets and proceeds, much like filing under a Chapter 13. It's used for very high amounts—the jurisdictional limits are $350,000 unsecured and $750,000 secured.

Coming out of bankruptcy is almost like entering the witness protection program, only you don't get set up in a new home with a new identity and credit rating. You also have no chance of a credit rating for at least ten years. Many people find it very difficult, if not impossible, to obtain a new mortgage, personal loan or even a credit card for years to come. When they do find a lender willing to give them another chance, they often receive less credit than desired, are charged higher interest rates, or pay much larger down payments. After ten years have passed, your chance at credit will improve; but it will be a slow recovery process.

Bankruptcy can be a mixed bag emotionally as well. Some who have gone through it feel a sense of relief that the nightmare of an increasing debt is no longer eating them alive. However, they also feel like they have been blacklisted from the consumer-oriented society to which we have all become accustomed. Counseling during this time period can be important as it helps the individual feel a sense of self-worth.

Some of your debts, such as child support, taxes, and student loans will remain after bankruptcy. However, you will be able to receive social security, disability, unemployment benefits, and in most cases, your pension.

Many people have, in time, successfully rebounded from bankruptcy and found themselves in lucrative careers and living very comfortable lifestyles. In fact, recent reports show that because consumers are increasingly more cautious of the money they borrow, there has been a reduction in personal bankruptcies. The American Bankruptcy Institute reported that personal bankruptcies reached an all time high in 1998 with 1.4 million filings. In 1999, the number had dropped to 1.3 million.

Bankruptcy cases must be filed in federal court. The filing fee is $160 which does not include other legal fees incurred by your lawyer.

Questions to Ask a Bankruptcy Attorney

- Do you practice bankruptcy law exclusively?
- How well-known are you in the local court system?
- Do you handle bankruptcy filings under Chapters 7, 11, and 13?
- Will you sit down with me to determine other alternatives or go straight to bankruptcy as the answer?
- Have you ever been a bankruptcy trustee? (If so, it shows that he or she has been intricately involved in the process.)

chapter seven

How to Avoid Getting Into Debt Again

At this point, it is necessary to summarize all the major points that have been previously discussed. We all become victims of debt at one point or another, but taking action against it is the best defense. Once you have managed to climb out of the trenches, you won't want to fall back in the hole again. The keys to preventing the situation from occurring again are simple, though not always easy to follow through with.

1. **Stick to the budget:** Once you have made the final payment that ends your debt, it is time to re-evaluate the budget you created at the start. At this point, there may be better ways to disperse your money. You may want to allocate a larger sum to your savings account

each week, or you may want to start investing for your retirement. Whatever you decide, know the plan and stick to it.

2.   **Pay bills on time:** This is probably one of the most important steps on which to focus. It can not be stressed enough. When a bill comes in, pay the total balance and your interest will not become an issue again.

3.   **Reconsider additional sources of income:** If you had decided to take another job to help make ends meet, you may want to consider keeping it for a while longer. The extra money you earn could be put towards savings, or it could be used to reward yourself for managing to break free of debt. An island vacation or a new wardrobe, *paid in cash*, may be a nice way to celebrate your success and keep you motivated for the future.

4.   **Ponder the plastic:** Now would also be the perfect time to take another look at the credit cards you are using. Is there a way to cut back even more on the use of these little devils? Which accounts are still open? Do you need them? Perhaps you could use one card instead of two. Maybe you should get rid of all those department store cards.

5.   **Cash, check, or charge?** As often as possible, pay by either cash, check, or use a debit card. Don't accrue credit card payments if you don't need to. Using one of these methods of payment makes you more aware of the money you are spending.

6.   **Plan for the future:** Put money away for the future. Start a savings account. Look into investment opportunities. Prepare for emergencies and make sure you can manage to live comfortably when you

retire. The next sections are designed to help you evaluate your options for the future. Living debt-free is a life-long commitment and requires a lot of planning along the way.

The Road To Tomorrow: The Importance of Saving

What's important about having and contributing to a savings account? To a small degree, you are allowing your money to work for you because you are earning interest on the balance (usually three to seven percent depending on the type of account). To a large degree, a savings account means peace of mind, whether you are in or out of debt. Keeping and building a savings account is crucial in laying a financial base for the future.

According to a report published by the Consumer Federation of America, 50 percent of American households have accumulated less than $1,000 in net financial assets. Research shows that millions of Americans are spending as much or more money than they make rather than taking advantage of available alternatives to building financial worth. Failure to save puts individuals and families at great financial risk and without resources to turn to in the event of emergency. Food for thought: Investing just $25 a week, for forty years, at a 7 percent annual yield would lead to a savings of close to $290,000. A little can sure go a long way.

A savings account becomes very important in the event of an emergency. It always seems that the brakes on the car need replacing at the worst possible time. Wouldn't it be nice to have the cash to pay for the repairs? Okay, it may not be fun to shell out $600 to the mechanic, but at least the cost has been paid in its entirety and you don't have to worry about the bill coming in later.

Here are some easy steps to help you with your quest to build a savings account:

1. Consider your savings account a monthly fixed expense. Think of it as paying yourself every month.

2. A penny saved is a penny earned, as the old adage goes. The loose change in your pocket or purse is great for depositing into a coffee can or piggy bank. When it's full, run to the bank and deposit it. Spare change is often seen as a nuisance but instead of letting it annoy you, let it earn you more money.

3. Did you recently get a raise? Still working the second job you got to help pay off the bills? Take some or all of this extra income and put it into savings. You won't even miss it.

Certificates of Deposit (CDs)

Once you have managed to save a substantial amount (around $1,500 or more), take $1,000 and lock it into a CD (certificate of deposit). CDs allow you to secure the same interest rate for a fixed amount of time, and the principle will not fluctuate. Through your bank or a credit union, you can purchase CDs for three months, six months, one year, or longer. Naturally, the longer you commit to with your CD, the higher your yield will be. On the other side of the equation is the early withdrawal penalty, should you cash in the CD before it is due. CDs are a good short-term no-risk place to invest money while you investigate longer term plans. They are a great way to "play it safe," particularly because they are insured by the FDIC.

Banks usually set a low minimum and so do not charge for the purchase of the certificate. Interest rates will vary depending on the bank, the amount of money, and the time frame you specify. Some banks even allow for designer CDs, which let you set the guidelines while the bank calculates the rate. Interest rate parameters are determined by the banks in conjunction with the current and expected future demand for loans.

The annual percentage yield on your CD is what the CD will earn on an annual basis, combining the stated rate of interest and the compounded frequency. Annual yields generally run between 3 and 7 percent, depending on whether you purchase a six-month, one-year, or five-year CD. Not to rain on your CD parade, but the interest from a CD is taxable.

Among the places to scout CDs are the major money and investing newspapers and magazines including the *Wall Street Journal*, *USA Today*, *Money Magazine*, *Barron's*, and *Kiplinger's Personal Finance Magazine*.

Retirement Plans

It's never too late or too early to start investing for your future. Sock money away into a retirement plan. Estimating how much money you will need to live on when you retire is not an easy task. But, there are numerous ways to go about ensuring a sizable nest egg for your golden years. How much money you need depends on your lifestyle, age at retirement, future plans, and other investments. It is estimated that you will need about 75 percent of your average income in your peak earning years, traditionally your forties and fifties. Naturally, this also depends on what you do for a living. The bottom line in determining your retirement expenses is to look at your current budget and see how much you need to cover your expenses at present. Then evaluate what expenses you will have at the age in which you plan to retire. Don't forget to increase the amount slightly in conjunction with the inflation rate.

It is not hard to set up a budget for your senior years if you look at what your current budget is and make appropriate adjustments. For example, you won't be paying for daily transportation to and from work, but you may need more money for weekly commuting to medical appointments. Likewise, family expenses for children may be much less, but you may need money for travel expenses to visit your grandchildren. Try to estimate your expenses. Then, take your total and multiply by the inflation factor. Inflation rates do fluctuate from year to year. A safe estimation would be to account for five percent inflation each year. For more information on calculating these figures, you may want to check out the following Web sites.

http://moneycentral.msn.com
www.usatoday.com/money/calculat/retirec.htm
http://personal300.fidelity.com/toolbox/retirecalc/frame.html

Start to save for retirement sooner rather than later. The primary options when it comes to setting up retirement accounts include 401(k), IRA, SEP-IRA, and Keogh accounts. Then there are also defined benefit plans, profit sharing, and other lesser known plans which we need not go into here.

401(k) Plans

Since their inception in 1981, the 401(k) plans have made saving for retirement particularly easy. Your employer sets up the account for you, and (if you choose to participate) your money is automatically transferred into it. Also, since you never see the money (contributions are usually made through salary deductions), you don't miss it, and you don't pay income taxes on it. Each employer may set up 401(k) plans differently, with some kicking in immediately and others going into effect after you have worked for the company for six months to a year. There are also stipulations regarding the number of hours you need to work.

As of 2001, you can contribute up to a maximum of $10,500 of your salary into a 401(k). In addition, the amount you contribute cannot exceed 15 percent of your salary. These are federal tax code regulations and do not vary by state, employer, or retirement plan company. Plan providers can set up other specifications in conjunction with the company. In over 80 percent of companies with such plans, employers match a portion of the amount you put in by 25, 40, 50, or even (though rarely) 100 percent. Some plans are vested, meaning that you need to stay for a certain number of years before you can benefit from the company-matched portion of the plan. Thus, companies are saying that they will help you save up for your retirement provided you stay with them for a designated period of time.

A 401(k) also gives you the flexibility to choose how you want your money invested. Plans generally offer a few options including money market accounts, general growth, or equity stock funds, or even stock in your own company. Different plans offer different options. Most of the time you can change these investments or the percentage of money allocated to each area.

Since 401(k) plans are for retirement, the one major restriction you have is that you must leave the money in the account until you are 59½ years of age, or face a stiff penalty upon withdrawal. However, in the case of some hardship situations, you can withdraw the money sooner without paying a penalty.

All in all, if a 401(k) plan is offered, you would be foolish not to participate. Reports show that in offices where such a plan is set up, more than half of the employees utilize it, and the number really should be higher. You do not pay tax on your 401(k) contributions, so if the company is matching your contribution at 50 percent, it's like getting at least 50 percent return on your investment.

For nonprofit organizations such as schools and hospitals, a 403(b) plan may be available. Although this tax sheltered plan is more limited in its investment options, it works on a similar basis to the 401(k) plan. Local and state governments offer a 457 plan. Roll overs on 457 plans may be restricted under state laws.

Roll Over

If you change jobs, either by choice or otherwise, you can roll over your 401(k) plan into the new company's plan; by law the employer has to allow you to do so. Or, you can roll the money into a rollover IRA account. It is to your advantage to have the money rolled over by a direct trustee-to-trustee transfer, thus avoiding any taxes. If you have the money sent directly to you, prior to putting it in to another account, the company has to withhold 20 percent in a new account or the money will be considered taxable income. If you can compensate for the 20 percent withheld from taxes when you open the new account, then none of the roll over will be taxable, thereby allowing the 20 percent that was withheld to be returned to you.

For example, if you receive $50,000, a withholding tax of $10,000 will be taken out, and you will receive a Form 1099 from the plan, showing the $50,000 distribution, with $10,000 withheld. If you then invest the remaining $40,000 into a rollover IRA within 60 days, only the $10,000 withheld (from the original $50,000) will be taxed. You will, therefore, pay a tax on $10,000 based on your income tax bracket (and a 10 percent penalty if you are under age 59½) and receive the balance as a refund. If, however, you deposit another $10,000 into the rollover IRA, to bring your total back up to $50,000 (within sixty days), there will be no taxable income and no tax. Upon filing your tax return with Form 1099 attached, you will be refunded the $10,000 that was withheld.

IRAs

For those who want to save for retirement but are not offered a 401(k) or 403(b) plan through their employer, IRAs are another option. IRAs (Individual Retirement Accounts) became the fashionable retirement plan over the course of the last decade. IRAs come in many configurations, but the bottom line is that you can contribute up to $2,000 a year. A non-working spouse may contribute an additional $2,000 a year.

Banks, mutual fund companies, and brokerage houses are some of the places from which you can obtain an IRA. The choice largely depends on your comfort level with the institution and their investment possibilities. Mutual fund families traditionally have more options, but banks, because of the competition, are now also offering a great number of ways in which you can invest. Brokerage houses can be the best places to turn because they can move your IRA from one fund to another very easily, without additional fees; and they often get good rates.

Withdrawing Money from a Traditional IRA

It's been mentioned before, but it's worth mentioning again. You can not withdraw money from an IRA without penalty until you have reached the age of 59½. Like everything else in life, there are exceptions. These exceptions include money used for qualifying higher education, first-time home buying expenses, or substantial medical costs. Also, if you inherit the IRA from your spouse and maintain the distribution schedule of the deceased spouse or if you have certain disabilities that can be expected to last indefinitely, you can withdraw money without a penalty.

Once you hit 59½, it's up to you to withdraw your money as you see fit. It helps to have a plan for withdrawing the money. Traditionally, once you hit 70½ it is mandatory that you start withdrawing your money, or you will face a stiff penalty.

Should you be holding a traditional IRA, the required annual withdrawal will be based on life expectancy depending on your age as determined by a government table (beginning at 70½ years of age). You need the total of the fair market value of all plan assets on the last day of the year and the appropriate divisor (based on age) from the government life expectancy table to calculate the amount of withdrawal for the current calendar year. If you do not meet the annual withdrawal amount minimum, you will pay a penalty of 50 percent of the amount you failed to withdraw.

If you are married, you can use a joint life expectancy table, which has a longer life expectancy than if you calculate for one person. If you use this double life expectancy, you have a higher divisor and lesser amount that you have to take out than if you use the single table.

If a person passes away, the spouse can roll over the IRA as the beneficiary. He or she may then continue taking the money out utilizing his or her own life expectancy of the joint life expectancy table if a "time certain" method of calculation was elected prior to the first withdrawal. A "time certain" method defines the number of years you are going to be making withdrawals in accordance with the government table.

Roth IRAs

A popular and relatively new type of IRA is the Roth IRA. The Roth is not unlike the traditional IRA in terms of getting a plan started. But you cannot take a deduction on a Roth as you can with the traditional IRA. However, with the Roth there are advantages on the withdrawal end that are significant. The maximum contribution on a Roth IRA is phased out for a single individual if the adjusted gross income (AGI) is between $95,000 and $110,000 and for a married couple if the AGI is between $150,000 and $160,000. *(This was the most current information at press time.)*

If your AGI is under $100,000, you may be able to roll over the money from your traditional IRA into a Roth IRA, but you will be taxed on the rollover. If you recently opened a traditional IRA and the amount is low, you may wish to pay the tax so that you can have the advantages on the withdrawal end of the Roth IRA. However, if you have had an IRA for years, the tax may be too high to make a rollover worth while. Also, as taxes are evaluated and debated in Congress over the ensuing years, it might be advantageous to wait and see what changes are made. Just as the Roth IRA recently appeared, you may find a newer model without rollover tax rates.

The Roth stipulates that money remain in the plan until you are 59½. After five years, you can withdraw money without a penalty if you are disabled, if you use the distribution to pay up to $10,000 of qualifying first-time home buying expenses, or if the distribution is to the beneficiary following the death of the account owner.

Seem confusing? Well, it is. But, keep in mind the primary difference between a traditional IRA and a Roth IRA boils down to a question of now or later. Would you prefer to take a tax deduction now and to pay taxes later upon the withdrawal, or would you prefer no deduction now but no taxes later? Evaluate this by your own current income level and tax bracket. Also consider what your income will be upon retirement. All in all, either a traditional or a Roth IRA is a strong retirement vehicle.

SEP and Simple IRAs

Two other IRAs are the SEP-IRA for people who are self-employed and the simple IRA for small businesses with incomes under $60,000. The SEP allows you to contribute 15 percent of your earned income up to $30,000; the Simple allows you to contribute up to the first $6,000 of earned income. These accounts are both light in paperwork. SEP-IRA plans may be established and contributions made for a tax year up until the return is filed, which may be October 15th for a return on extension.

IRA Inertia

The vast majority of IRA holders do little, if anything, with their IRAs, beyond the annual contribution. The thinking is that once the money is earmarked for retirement, worry about it later. This isn't necessarily a bad thing. If you are earning a good rate of interest, you need not take the time and effort to seek out a tenth of a point higher interest in some other type of account. Often people find themselves chasing returns based on reading an article or hearing about a hot fund that may have been a bigger winner last year. Unfortunately, the hot fund one year may not be the next year's winner. If you are going to take an active interest in your IRA or in your finances in general, do your homework and don't be impulsive. Study the trends over a period of time and don't jump on the latest return. Return chasing can be as hazardous as chasing tornadoes.

On the other hand, don't let your IRA languish if you are getting a low rate of return or have money in cash accounts that won't help you reach your ultimate financial goals. You can keep an eye out for better interest rates and move your IRA accordingly. The same holds true with your level of risk. If you are more comfortable taking a greater risk than you were when you started the IRA or if you now need to save for your new-born son or daughter's college tuition in eighteen years, you might want to take a higher risk approach.

Keogh Plans

In a Keogh plan, employers set aside money for themselves and their employees. After three years of work, at 1,000 hours or more per year, employees must be deemed eligible for coverage. Keogh plans, however, are most popular with those that are self-employed. You are allowed a maximum contribution as a self-employed individual of $30,000 per year. There are three types of Keogh plans, and additional constraints may be imposed depending on the type of plan.

In a **profit sharing Keogh**, annual contributions are limited to 15 percent but can also be as low as 0 percent in a given year. In a **money purchase Keogh**, contributions are limited to 1 to 25 percent of compensation (but once set, they must continue for the life of the plan). A **paired Keogh** combines the terms of the profit sharing and money purchase plans. Keogh plans must be established by December 31st of the year for which you want to start making contributions, although you have until you file your tax return (which can be October 15th if on an extension) to make the contribution.

Like IRA and 401(k) plans, Keoghs have the penalties for early withdrawal, or money taken out of the account before the age of 59½. Once you retire, you can have the money paid to you in monthly amounts (which are taxable) or in one lump sum (which is also taxable). Also, like the other plans, distributions must start by age 70½.

Since self-employment or any employment situation may change, you can roll over the money into an IRA. The roll over rules are similar to those of the 401(k) plan; a direct trustee-to-trustee transfer is recommended to avoid having to pay any taxes.

The SEP (which was discussed earlier) is a variation on the Keogh; it can be easier to administer than the typical pension plan and beneficial to small businesses. Employers and employees both put money into this plan.

Other Types of Plans

In a **profit sharing plan**, the company for whom you work pools a specific amount of its profits and distributes them annually according to a set formula. If the company does not show a profit or shows a very small profit, less money is put into the plan.

A **money purchase plan** works in a similar manner, only the amount is not based on profits but on your salary. These plans are less common because if the company does not show a profit, it still must make the contribution to its employees.

Retirement plans are usually tax deferred, which makes them attractive. Unless you are self-employed or are an employer, you will have little to say about which plan your company offers. However, you should participate if such a retirement plan is made available to you.

Equity

We have discussed equity before, but now it is time to examine it in a different context. Once you have managed to overcome debt, it is a good time to look at other ways to make your money and assets work to your advantage. Taking a closer look at the things you own and how you spend your money may help you to find alternative ways to capitalize on your situation.

Most of us are not collectors of antiques or fine art. Let's face it: Who can afford such things? You won't see Joe Smith selling off a Rembrandt when he reaches retirement, or Susie Anderson auctioning off the Tiffany lamp purchased in Paris. However, it is not far fetched that Joe or Susie may own houses that offer a great source of equity (defined as simply the value of the property).

If you and your spouse are rattling around a nine-room house, you might decide to sell and buy a retirement condo in Florida or Arizona for half the price of what the house sold for. If you do, you will have gained that much extra for your retirement years. The current government home equity tax laws allow you to sell your home and not pay tax on up to $250,000 profit as a single individual or $500,000 if you are married. You had to have lived in the house for a minimum of only two years.

The scenario is not uncommon. Often couples, as well as widows or widowers, find that they are happier in a new setting during their retirement years and that they no longer need a large house. They may, in fact, no longer need two cars. It's not a matter of cutting back, it's a matter of being comfortable and practical. Larger houses mean more to take care of and more to clean. Two cars mean more money for maintenance and for insurance payments. For many people reaching retirement age, it's a matter of practicality. Your home is, therefore, a major asset that you might use to your advantage.

chapter eight

Handling Money During Retirement

If you have done some proper planning in advance, you should be able to enjoy your retirement years while resting assured that you have money available to you. While it is likely that your living expenses will be lower, you will still need to have some form of steady income. You've worked long and hard to get to this point; you should not have financial headaches during these twilight years.

As always, you will need to figure out a budget in advance, as you did prior to retirement—the difference being that during retirement your income will be derived from money withdrawn from those retirement plans that you set up, plus Social Security and any pension you are entitled to. You might also think about part-time work to remain busy as well as save some money. If you are able to equal 75 percent of your income prior to retirement then you should do fine.

During the five to ten years approaching retirement, you should set up your plan. Think about these questions:

1. What do you want to be doing during retirement?
2. Where do you want to be living?
3. What finances will be available to you and your spouse?

Your anticipated lifestyle will have a lot to do with planning your financial future. The couple who wants to spend a great deal of time traveling might want a smaller permanent location. They may want to spend more money on airline tickets and other such travel expenses and less money on home repair and maintenance.

The couple who wants to maintain their home and have their children and grandchildren there often to visit might look for local activities to become involved with in order to stay active. It's long been theorized that people who stay active live longer, more enriched lives.

Five Retirement Options to Consider

Many of the financial magazines, the planners, and the experts offer a host of new and inventive ways to invest your money. If you've worked many years to save up for retirement or you are trying to get by on a more limited amount of income/savings, this is not the time to get caught up in anything risky. However, with inflation, an approach that is too safe and conservative may have you falling behind.

Here are some suggestions you should try and consider, depending on how much money you are dealing with, your age, and your lifestyle. Remember, your goal is to be comfortable with the money you have coming in.

1. Keep at least the first $30,000 in a safe place, such as a bank CD, Treasury note, money market account, or other cash instrument. Yes, this may sound boring, but if this is your cushion, you need to hold on to it with a tight grasp.

2. Invest a high percentage of your portfolio in bond funds (through a broker or planner). If you want a steady stream of income, investing in high yield bond funds is one way to achieve it. These funds can provide a cushion you won't find with more high-risk equity funds.

3. Sell off the house, buy a condo, and put your money toward travel, grandchildren, and other things you desire. Many retirees appreciate not having to pay real estate taxes and maintenance on a house that is way too large for them. Put the rest of the money into investments, starting with safe ones and expanding to more risky ones based on your needs and how much money you have to work with.

4. Convert cash value life insurance into an annuity plan that pays monthly income. The money that built up during your working years when your family needed to be supported can now be better invested.

5. Keep an active portfolio. Again, this depends on your income and amount saved. However, if you have had a retirement plan—401(k) or pension— or accumulated any significant savings, you can

maintain a diversified portfolio, only hedge toward the more conservative side. Equities can work in your favor, particularly those paying dividends; just maintain the percentage of your money in stock funds or individual equities that makes you feel comfortable.

Some Helpful Retirement Planning Web Sites

American Express Retirement Services
(www.americanexpress.com/401k)

Focuses on 401(k) plans and how they work. The site provides easy to understand information about calculating the amount you need to invest to reach your desired goals.

Social Security Retirement Planner
(www.ssa.gov/retire)

Provides information on all areas of planning for retirement, including a calculator for figuring out finances.

T. Rowe Price
(www.troweprice.com/retirement)

Offers concise, easy-to-follow listings and explanations of the many retirement options from IRAs to more complex plans for small business owners.

chapter nine

A Few Words on Personal Borrowing and Lending

Besides borrowing money from the bank against the equity of your home or retirement account, you can also consider borrowing money from friends and family. Naturally, there are no set guidelines and no Web sites designed to give you the best interest rates among family members. Only you will be able to determine from whom you feel comfortable borrowing money. Below are a few friendly pointers.

Here are some important considerations when borrowing from family and friends:

- Look to borrow money from people you know to be financially sound. Thus, you can avoid the awkward situation in which someone says, "I'd love to lend you the money, but I don't have it myself."

- Borrow money only for specific targeted needs; be sure you will be able to pay it back.
- Write up an agreement, no matter how basic, detailing how much money you are borrowing and when you anticipate paying it back.
- From time to time, remind the lender that you are aware of the loan.
- Pay off the loan as soon as you possibly can.
- Money has come between many friends. The best intentions have led to feuding even among the closest of pals. Money has a strange effect on people. If you feel that someone has a very different outlook regarding money than you do, this may not be the person you want to borrow from. Personalities vary and so do outlooks regarding money. Many people will lend money without interest due. These same people may then, in a subtle, often unconscious manner, become controlling. Money lent with emotional strings attached can be harder to pay off than money lent with interest due. Once again, know your lender and make sure both sides fully understand the agreement before going through with the loan.

Lending Money

In the event that you are in the position of lending money to someone, there are two simple rules of thumb to follow. First, if you can not afford to lend it, don't. Second, if you do lend the money, treat it like an investment; you may or may not recoup it. If you go into the lending process with that attitude, you won't be disappointed if you don't see it again. Even when a lending company imparts money, they are very aware that there is a great amount of risk involved. For this reason, they look for collateral. It's more difficult for most people, however, to say to a friend, "Give me your watch, and if you pay back the money, I'll return it to you." If you ask for interest, spell out in writing exactly what interest rate you are seeking. But always be reasonable.

You may also be asked to help someone out by paying off a debt for them, rather than handing the money directly to them. You can then set up an arrangement for them to pay you back. Work with your friend to develop the plan in the same way that you developed and implemented your own plan for getting out of debt. Now that the shoe is on the other foot, try to be sympathetic to the needs and struggles of your friend or family member.

It is often recommended that you base both lending and borrowing on standard business operating procedures. This means, you look at what banks and other lending institutions are doing and, in a simplified manner, follow some of their procedures. For example, you could follow their procedure in regard to a term loan or an installment loan. With a term loan, you pay the loan back in one lump sum at a lower interest rate. With an installment loan, you pay it off gradually, usually at a higher rate of interest. Or you could simply agree on the going interest rate and then collect the money in monthly, weekly, or biweekly installments.

chapter ten

Learning to Shop Smart for Big Purchases

Car Buying

In this day and age cars have become necessary conveniences of everyday life. If you are at the point where you need to purchase a car, it is to your advantage to arm yourself with as much information as possible. Figure out beforehand how much you can afford to spend in monthly payments and make it clear to the dealer that you can not go over that amount. Car salespersons are notorious for the hard sell, and many consumers end up getting more than they bargain for when buying a vehicle. You want to ensure that purchasing this vehicle isn't going to put you in the poor house and back in debt. The bottom line is that a number of things have to fall in line before you make this major purchase.

- Make sure that the car meets but does not exceed your current needs. If you can live without the CD player, do so and save yourself a few hundred dollars. A larger car for a family or a smaller car for a single person may be in order.
- Look at various features such as gas mileage, trunk space, leg room, acceleration, and handling. Make a checklist that includes features of significance to you.
- Be ready to haggle, negotiate, and haggle some more, and if necessary go elsewhere—car dealerships are a dime a dozen. Try not to jump at the first sporty car you see. Shop around and get the best deal. A car is not an impulse buy and should never be the result of a high pressure sales pitch.
- Find out about the warranty. Usually the manufacturer gives the warranty for three to five years or for up to a certain number of miles. Look closely at what the warranty covers. The power train, including transmission and engine, are most important. Also, be careful in regard to extended warranties offered by the dealership. They will try to make you purchase these and often they are an unnecessary added expense. You might sell the car before the warranty even kicks in.
- Consider financing. Can you buy a new car outright or will you be paying it off? If you will be financing the car, it's to your advantage to have a line of credit available to you through a bank or other lending institution. You can often finance directly through the dealer but this can end up being more costly.
- Determine whether a new or used car is a more valuable purchase than repairing your present car. A new car is an expense, not an investment. A car, unlike a house, will not become more valuable over time, unless you

keep the car in good working condition until it is no longer made and becomes an antique. For most of us though, cars will depreciate as time passes beginning with the moment you drive it off the lot. In fact, most cars will depreciate by 25 percent during the first year. (A car purchased for $18,000 would likely be worth $13,500 or less in that short amount of time.)

- Take a test drive. It is very important to test drive any vehicle you are thinking of buying. See that the car does not drift to one side, that the alignment is straight, that the steering is easy and smooth, that the brakes work smoothly and quickly at a variety of speeds, that the sight lines are good (no major blind spots), that there are no unusual sounds. When you are finished, check the engine and look under the car to see that there are no leaks. The bottom line is that you should make up a list of all the functions and check them out in a test drive.

- Seriously consider having a mechanic double check the car. Mechanics can often find the things you may have missed or simply overlooked.

- When you are ready to buy, look over the paperwork very carefully, especially the fine print. Then make sure you obtain the title forms and proper registration. Also, make sure you have the proper auto insurance, which is required in most states.

Financing a New Car

Paying cash for a new car may sound absurd to some. After all, where are you going to come up with an extra $16,000 to $25,000? However, if you consider that you save for the down payment on a home, college tuition, a wedding, and retirement, you can see exactly where the money can come from. Much in the way you will pay off a car (through monthly payments with an interest rate), you can set aside the money (without the interest rate) and save up to buy a car outright. In fact, the money will actually grow, and you will be saving significantly if you can set aside money in a new-car account.

Don't despair if you have to play the auto finance game. BUT, do your homework. Keep in mind that additional costs, beyond financing (the loan and interest), can include fees for paperwork and credit reports.

Other car costs, before you even hit the road, will include insurance and licensing fees. Then comes the cost of maintaining the car. Warranties will help with repair costs, but gas and regular maintenance are both line items for your budget. Regular maintenance includes checking the oil, antifreeze, tires, belts, hoses, wipers, and so forth, and will help keep your car in good condition in the long run. And finally, don't forget to add the inspection fee to your car expense list.

Buying a Used Car

Used cars have been very much in vogue in the nineties. If you are careful, shop wisely, and have the car checked out, you can often get a good deal with a car that has been owned before. No longer are all used car dealers the stereotypical wheeler dealer types who try to squeeze you into a lemon. In fact, there are now giant used-car conglomerates, such as CarMax and AutoNation USA, that offer a wide selection of used cars in one huge outlet.

There are also numerous smaller dealers coast to coast who sell "late model" cars off their lots. If you buy a car off the lot, be sure to scout around and get some firsthand accounts from other satisfied customers. Get a feel for the reputation of the dealership. Also, find out about trade-ins. Trade-in allowances for your current car can often be in the area of 20 to 25 percent off the price of the car you buy.

The advantage of buying a used car is, obviously, that you will be saving money. You do still have to pay sales tax on the car, but it will be less than that for a new car.

The first step naturally, is to find the car you want. The National Association of Automobile Dealers issues an *Official Guide to Used Cars*; this guide lists the going rate for the year and model of every car. Another informative site worth checking out comes from *Kelley Blue Book (www.kbb.com)*. Here you will find car values for new and used vehicles as well as financing information. Ultimately, you will have to be the final judge. No matter what the book says or what the odometer reads, you have to feel completely comfortable with the condition and price of the car.

Home Buying

Major purchases such as a home, other real estate, or a car usually require a great deal of involvement with the bank. Therefore, your first order of business is to find a bank that you feel comfortable dealing with and one that feels comfortable dealing with you.

When planning a major purchase, you should once again review your assets and look over your budget very carefully, since this new purchase will have a long-lasting impact on how and where a large portion of your money will be allocated. You will want this major purchase to fit nicely into the scheme of your life at the time. So make sure there are not other things that need to be addressed first. If you didn't get that raise you were counting on, your son needs braces, you're saving for your daughter's college tuition, or the leaky roof needs repair, you might decide that you are just not able to purchase that new three-bedroom home in the suburbs.

The First Steps

Now that you are in a position to buy a home, prepare to be overwhelmed by the experience. Many people are afraid they simply can't afford a new home and will never be approved for a loan. Often this is not the case, but remember that each person's financial situation is different. Be sure that you have gone over your budget carefully before deciding to make such a commitment. You would not want to make a purchase that is going to put you immediately back in debt after you worked so hard to get out of it. You have to do what is right for you at the present time.

The Mortgage Bankers Association of America (MBA) suggests that you first talk to an accredited real estate loan officer. For the most part, loan officers will be more than happy to answer your questions because they want your business. Loan officers can act as consultants, offering help and various plans. People should not be afraid to go in with questions and establish a relationship even before seeking approval. Go to more than one bank and don't be discouraged if one paints a less than rosy picture. You should seek out as much information as you can by checking the real estate sections of the newspaper and even by attending seminars.

One common myth regarding home mortgages is that home buyers (especially those purchasing for the first time) need a spotless credit reference. Often people worry even if they have missed a single credit card payment by thirty days. Others worry because they don't have a credit card. In such cases, banks look at utility bill payments, water bills, and even rent payments. All you have to do is travel across America to see that millions of people, from all walks of life and from all income levels, live in their own homes. So, obviously finding and financing a home is something that is done every day.

Another myth is that a 20 to 30 percent down payment is required to purchase a home. However, many homes are purchased with 10 percent down, some with as little as 5 percent. Naturally, the more money you put down, the less you will have to pay off in a mortgage.

When planning to purchase a home, there are several areas you must be familiar with. For example, you should know the difference between fixed-rate mortgages and adjustable rate mortgages. There is also the matter of determining how much you can afford to spend. As a general rule, the theory is that you should anticipate spending two and a half times your annual family income on your home. Thus, a family earning $50,000 a year would likely consider purchasing a home in the $100,000 to $125,000 price range. Of course, this will vary based on savings and debts. And there are special loan programs available that allow couples to buy homes at even higher prices.

Help for first-time home buyers is available from the Federal Housing Administration and the Rural Housing and Community Development Service. You may qualify for loans from these two government offices. You may also be eligible for a VA loan if you have been or are currently serving in the armed forces. Many other groups and organizations offer assistance for first-time home buyers.

The Process

Once you have decided to go house hunting, you should get what is called preapproval. To determine whether you will be approved for a mortgage once you find the home you like, the bank looks over all of your financial records, including tax returns and income statements. This process is becoming increasingly important because brokers often do not want to start showing you houses until they know that you have a range of prices that you can afford (preapproval will help you determine the amount at which you can buy a house).

According to Fannie Mae, the nation's largest source of home mortgage funds, no more than 36 percent of your income should go to mortgage payments. This includes interest and the escrow deposits for real estate tax. This rule is not fixed in stone; it is merely a guideline that brokers use. Therefore, if you earn a combined income of $100,000, you should be able to spend $36,000 a year or $3,000 a month on your mortgage and escrow deposit. Some banks and lenders are more conservative, expecting you to spend only 25 percent of your income on your home expenses.

Mortgages

There are several types of mortgages you can get from lenders. It's important that you choose both the lender and the mortgage carefully, since your home mortgage (and subsequent payments) will be part of your life for a long time, sort of like a guest who comes to visit and never leaves.

In your mortgage search, you will discover several places from which you can borrow. Carefully explore what each one offers before even applying. Direct lenders such as savings banks, commercial banks, and savings and loans are very popular in the mortgage market. Mortgage brokers have recently become the choice of many home shoppers. They are especially helpful for people with credit problems, those who are self-employed, and anyone who doesn't have a lot of time to shop around.

Choices, Choices, and More Choices

Do you want a 15-, 20-, or 30-year mortgage? The basic rule of thumb is that the shorter the term of the loan, (or mortgage in this case), the lower the amount of interest you will have to pay. On the other hand, the shorter the term, the higher the monthly payments. The amount of your down payment will enter into your decision regarding the length of term of your mortgage. At present, 10 percent is a common down payment.

Mortgage Loans in a Nutshell

Once upon a time there were just fixed-rate and adjustable-rate loans. Now a whole set of new options have come forth to confuse and overwhelm the home buyer. Here is a brief description of each to help you gain an idea of which may be the best choice for you.

Thirty-year fixed-rate mortgage: A good way to go for those who like stability and plan to stay in the same place for a while. It's been the loan for millions of home owners. You pay a fixed-rate for thirty years and when it's over, you throw a party and burn the mortgage. It's the tried and true loan for those who don't want to be bothered following interest rates.

Fifteen-year fixed-rate mortgage: Along the same idea as the thirty-year; this mortgage has a lower interest rate but higher monthly payments.

Adjustable-rate mortgage (ARMs): With this type of mortgage, the rate is adjusted every year, three years, or five years, or whatever was decided upon the signing of the loan. Initially, the rates are lower than those of fixed-rate mortgage plans. The rates are compiled from the national mortgage average, which is compiled by the Federal Home Loan Bank, using a number of different sources including the prime lending rate and other factors. Just like with investing, the rates can go either way. For your protection, most ARMs include caps or maximums regarding how high your interest rates can go in a year or during the lifetime of the loan.

Fixed adjustable-rate mortgages: These loans are fixed for five, seven, or ten years and adjustable thereafter, either every year or every three or five years, depending on the loan. There are also loans that fluctuate for the initial years and become a fixed rate later on. These loans may be good for those who are not planning to stay in a house very long. The huge number of fixed-adjustable rates combinations work well for people who follow interest rates and are prepared to finance, if and when necessary.

Balloon mortgage rates: These are shorter term loans (usually five to ten years) that stipulate a series of equal payments, then balloon into a full payment at the end. The interest rate can be much lower, but you must have plans to refinance at the current rates once the loan is due. This is yet another option for people who are just getting started, young couples, or someone fresh out of school. It is also good option for someone who is not planning on staying in a home for long. (Home owners average just eight years in one home). The loan is then refinanced. Sometimes lenders set up refinancing plans at the time of the loan, but they usually won't lock you in at a particular rate.

Guaranteed payment mortgage: This type of mortgage is often good for young home buyers who expect their earnings to increase over the years. Your payments start low and gradually build over time along with your income level. The drawback of such a loan is that if your income does not increase, (or if it does but your expenses increase as well), the rising payments can be difficult.

Shared appreciation loans: These loans have a very low interest rate, but in return, the lender receives part of your home appreciation. Therefore, as the value of the home increases, so does the amount that is owed by the lender. These are not as common anymore because lenders aren't as comfortable predicting the real estate market as they were back in the '70s. Also, people don't like the idea of the lender owning a part of their home.

You and Your Credit Scores

Credit scores are used to evaluate your risk factor in loan application. Since lenders don't want to rely solely on their judgment, they now have a score card they can refer to. Actually it can help remove any bias or prejudice from the decision process.

Since 1955, credit scores have gained momentum—Fannie Mae and Freddie Mac have used them as a guide when evaluating mortgage applications. Although they are not the final word, they are now heavily considered. This rating system, endorsed by the Federal Reserve, has proven to be a fairly decent indicator of loan performance.

Refinancing

People decide to refinance when mortgage rates have dropped far enough that it is worth going through the hassle of the mortgage process all over again. Of course, if you do not intend on staying in a house for very long it may not be worth the trouble or aggravation to refinance. So, consider your future plans before going ahead with the refinancing process.

In order to refinance, you have to reapply, and with any luck, the value of your home will be attractive to the lender. There are a variety of charges associated with refinancing (not unlike getting the initial mortgage), so it is important to lower your mortgage enough to make these costs worthwhile. Do the math: divide the cost of refinancing by the monthly savings to figure out how long it will be until you are saving money. You should also review the tax laws in your state before deciding to refinance (or deciding on your mortgage for that matter).

It is also advised that you consider lenders other than the one you originally financed with. The idea that you will save on paperwork isn't usually valid, because in most cases, the loans have been sold and therefore new paperwork needs to be administered anyway. On the other hand, your original lender may not want to lose your business and if you have been a good customer, they may decide to forego some of the fees.

You can also "cash out" by refinancing for more than the principle due on your original loan. You get the cash that is left after the original mortgage is paid (less the closing costs), and since it is a loan it's tax free. Essentially, you are borrowing on the difference between the value of the house now versus the amount you owe on the original mortgage. This money can serve as a good source of funds for college tuition or for capital to start a business. However, cashing out won't work if the value of the house has decreased or stayed the same.

Home Equity Loans

You hear the term home equity often because it is another way for people to borrow money and pay interest. The interest rate is low because the collateral is your house. The process is similar to that of a second mortgage. Your house needs to be appraised, and there is plenty of other paperwork, plus some expenses, along the way. For the most part, the reason for taking out a home equity loan is a significant one, such as for home renovations or paying college tuition. Make sure it's a good reason. Don't ever use home equity in the same manner as using a credit card, or you will be putting yourself and your home in jeopardy.

Reading Mortgage Rate Sheets

Look for a loan that fits your needs. The 7/1 or other such breakdowns are the fixed-adjustable years in the loan. Thanks to daily financial pages, the Financial News Network, and the Internet, you should always be able to get the latest rates. The listing will also tell you the date through which the rate is available.

MORTGAGE RATE SHEET

LOAN PROGRAM	PERCENTAGE
30 year fixed rate	7.087
15 year fixed rate	6.893
15 year FHA loans	6.917
30 year FHA loans	7.440
1 year ARMs	6.010
3/1 year ARMs	6.555
7/1 year ARMs	7.091
7/23 year Balloon	6.787

Remember that lenders must follow guidelines. All costs, including lock-in, registration, and any other fees, must be included in your final quote. You should not be hit with additional closing costs. Get everything in writing ahead of time. You can also check with Mortgage Market Information Services (MMIS).

Tips for Home Buyers

- Don't be fooled by so-called low rates. Of course, the lower the better, but not at the expense of an unethical lender you do not trust; make sure there are no extra or hidden fees. You and your lender are going to be in business together for a long time. Make sure you are confident in their ability to keep your best interest in mind.
- Get everything in writing, including rate locks and other details. If you are preapproved for a mortgage, make sure you obtain the bank's conditions that must be fulfilled in order for the mortgage to go through. READ ALL CONTRACTS CAREFULLY.
- Make sure you and the person selling the home are independently represented. If the same person or agency is representing both sides, there may be a conflict of interest.
- Have an engineer inspect the home, including the roof, basement, grounds, and so forth. Even the most honest of sellers may be unaware of items in need of significant repair. Do not waive a clause by the seller to have the home inspected.
- Find out the amount of time that homes in the area—including the one you are looking at—have been on the market. You can usually start bidding at 15 percent below the asking price. BUT, if the houses in the neighborhood are going fast (say in two or three weeks), you may have to start at 7 or even 5 percent.

chapter eleven

Teach Your Children Well

The old adage, an ounce of prevention equals a pound of cure seems particularly appropriate when discussing the topic of debt. Children need to learn the value of money from their parents. It's a good idea to start teaching them at an early age. Starting as preschoolers, children can be given small amounts of money to spend on candy or a small toy. In this way, they will learn early that money is valuable and can be exchanged for other things. You can show them that their quarter can buy a gum ball or a piece of chocolate, but not both. From such simple examples, children can learn to appreciate that money means making choices.

As children reach school age, they can learn that money is used not only to buy toys and candy, but also to buy food, clothing, household items, and services. You can show a child at the market, or in any type of store, how you pay for things and how you get change back. As children see you spending money and making choices about where to spend it, they will begin to more fully understand its many uses.

It's also a good idea to bring your children with you to the bank to show them how money is kept safely. Be careful to explain ATM machines as places that *give you your own money*, much like the Pez dispenser gives you back the candy that you put into it. Otherwise children may believe that the ATM machine is a endless source of cash for you.

It's also important to explain how you obtain money by doing something to earn it. Bring Your Daughter to Work Day has become very popular. It shows young girls where their moms work and earn money. Obviously, this idea works equally well with fathers and sons, mothers and sons, or fathers and daughters. To further reinforce the lesson of doing something to earn money, you can reward children with small amounts of money for doing certain chores, such as cleaning up their rooms or washing the dishes.

Parents can also help develop a child's attitude toward money by including them in discussions and decisions regarding financial matters. If you explain to a child that a vacation and a new computer cost the same but that you only have enough money to pay for one, they can help the family decide. While details of the family economic picture are not for young children or even teenagers to evaluate, they can be part of the decision-making process when it comes to money spent on family matters.

First and foremost it is important to set a good example for the children in your household. Don't use money as a bribe to get the kids to do chores; instead make it a reward for hard work that they accomplished. Teach them the value of working for pay. Also, warn them against the dangers of credit. It's okay if Bobby needs to borrow some money from you; just make sure to set up a definitive repayment plan that has consequences if not fulfilled. This way kids are learning what the real world of money is all about.

Perhaps the best way for kids to learn is through an allowance system. Many parents are afraid that kids will not use their allowance wisely. Although kids can make some foolish spending choices, making the ultimate decision to buy their own things will help them to learn from their mistakes. Money is something children will have to deal with all through their lives. It is better to make mistakes earlier in life rather than later.

Once an allowance is instituted, it is important for the child to realize that there will not be any extra money given. If they want to go to the movies and they don't have enough cash, they won't be able to go. You may even consider helping your child develop a simple budget so that they can monitor the money they are spending.

Younger kids can further learn to appreciate the value of a dollar by starting their own small business (like a lemonade stand, baby-sitting, or dog walking). As children get older and can take on more responsibility, a part-time job will offer more opportunities. Encourage your child to save the money and work toward a long-term goal, such as the purchase of a new bicycle, skis, or even a used car.

Lastly, you should encourage your child to save money as soon as they start receiving an allowance. Open up a savings account with them. Work with them to develop a plan for saving. For example: You may decide that money given as a gift for birthdays and holidays will be divided up: half for spending and half in the savings account for the future (specifically college). You might be surprised by what your child decides to do. He or she may end up saving it all!

As hard as you try, you won't be the only one shaping your child's attitudes about money (or anything else for that matter).

Friends, teachers, relatives, and the media will also have an impact. But if you instill a good foundation for spending and saving, your child will likely be successful in money matters.

Here are some pointers to keep in mind:

- Do not be afraid to let your children make some mistakes along the way. If you scold them every time they spend money in a way you don't approve of, they may develop a bad attitude toward money. And besides, what adult hasn't made a spending mistake or two?
- Let them enjoy buying things as well as saving money. The first part is easy; the second may require a "game" approach. If they can enjoy both sides of the equation, they'll be more easily able to develop a sense of confidence in their money-related decision making.
- Let children's gift money belong to them. Parents should never use the money given to their children for themselves.
- Understand that children lose things, including money. If a small child loses a nickel or an older child loses a five dollar bill, you might replace it the first time. If it begins to happen with more frequency, you may need them to learn the hard way that the lost money is just that: lost. However, if your child complains of losing lunch money every day, even when you are certain it's in a safe place, find out if perhaps the child is being bullied into giving it to another child. This scenario occurs more often than you may care to think.
- Teach children at an early age not to take money from (or give money to) strangers.
- Don't get children involved in money fights at home. Money, as we all know, has a great deal of power attached to it. Children need not have all the responsibilities that go

along with the almighty dollar. They don't need to learn to equate money with power.

- Let children also recognize that money does not buy everything. When the opportunity presents itself, show them that something that is free, perhaps a day at the beach or park, can be better than something that requires spending money. It's a valuable lesson for all of us.

chapter twelve

The High Cost of Education: A Parent's Perspective

The average annual cost of college education has surpassed the $21,000 mark, and four-year public schools are approaching $10,000 a year, including room and board. At an annual increase of 5 percent per year (which seems to be average), college tuition for a child currently in kindergarten may be $50,000 or more per year for a private college and over $21,000 for a public university.

No matter how you slice it, a college education is going to cost lots and lots of money. Subsidizing the expense of higher education need not put parents and students in the poorhouse. There are a variety of ways to gain financial assistance if you qualify, and there are other resources such as scholarships and grants that can be looked into.

Not unlike a retirement plan, a college savings plan needs to build over a period of time and should be invested in on a regular basis. It is important to make a serious, committed effort to such a plan for it to work in the long run.

Projecting College Costs

Many books, magazines, and financial planners suggest first trying to assess what type of school your child will attend before starting your savings plan. This is no easy task when you are looking at your three-year-old watching cartoons. Instead, plan to save at least 75 percent of what the cost of the better schools will be when your child is ready to attend. You want the best for your child, so prepare for it. The saving will be tough but attainable if you plan early and then stick to the plan. Here are the main ways to reach your goal. As always, you have to find a plan that you are comfortable with and that will be affordable over time.

Invest: The amount of time you have before your children are ready for college will determine your investment flexibility. If you start when your child is three, you can utilize the potential of the long-term stock market and stock mutual funds. If your child is ten or eleven, you will need to think more in terms of bond funds and other low-risk means of building a portfolio. Whatever you plan, as your child nears college, you may progressively move more of your money into safer investments.

Savings Bonds: Series EE savings bonds can be cashed in and used for college tuition, tax free, if done in the same year. There are several requirements including income restrictions before the tax-free part comes into play. For example, the bond must be in the name of one or both parents, not in the child's name. However, even without the tax breaks, EE bonds are safe investments. Although they tie up your money for at least five years, they are always purchased at a discount from the face value of the bond. The rate of interest varies, but it is currently around 6 percent, if you hold the bond for five or more years.

Some federally tax-exempt college bonds are offered by individual states to increase state college enrollment. These bonds pay a fixed interest rate that is set at the time of purchase. The advantage is that colleges in these states offer a tuition discount based on the redemption of these bonds. If your son or daughter, however, chooses to go to school out of state, you will still be cashing in a viable bond, but you won't receive the discount.

Mutual Funds For Tuition: If your child is under ten, which gives you at least seven years until college, you can start off more aggressively by playing the popular mutual fund game with some of (but not all of) your college tuition plan. Choose a solid-growth oriented mutual fund and let the stock market work for you. Again, as your student gets into his/her second or third year of high school, start moving more of this money into shorter term, safer investment plans. Balanced mutual funds will diversify some of that money between stocks and bonds, providing you with an even safer investment.

Zero Coupon Bonds for Tuition: If you have the money, (most people do not) you might opt to buy zero coupon bonds. A $10,000 bond bought when your child is five years old (earning in the neighborhood of 7 to 8 percent with twelve years to maturity) will be worth about $22,000 when it matures and he or she is ready for college.

Zero coupon bonds are issued by the U.S. government, private companies, or municipalities. The *zero* indicates that you are receiving zero interest until the bond matures, at which point you will receive all the accumulated interest at one time at a rate set when you purchase it. This can help alleviate your concern about fluctuating interest rates or reinvesting interest. In essence you know when you buy a zero coupon bond exactly how much it will pay at the time it matures, and these rates are fairly good, since banks don't have to worry about paying you interest along the road to maturity. Other bonds can also work for you. Just be sure to keep track of the bond rates.

Cash Value Life Insurance Plans For Tuition: Some cash value life insurance plans allow you to cash them in for money. This is generally not a good way to build up the kind of funds needed to help defer the high costs of college. You can do much better with mutual funds, bonds, or other investment plans.

Prepaid Tuition Plans: Several states allow you to start paying your children's college when they are very young, usually under five years old. Although there are great discounts offered, this is a long-term risk, as your child may not be thrilled with having had these choices made before he or she was old enough to speak. If this happens, you will get a refund but it may not be 100 percent of the amount you spent. Also, you could invest the same money elsewhere, and it would grow (which is in actuality what the college is doing).

529 Plan: There are two types of 529 plans. The first is a prepaid tuition plan that guarantees that the money you contribute will grow at the same inflation rate as state-run college tuitions. This money can be used at a state school located somewhere other than the state whose plan you use.

The second type is a savings plan. You put your money into an investment pool, which may grow at a rate faster than the tuition inflation rate. This is a slightly riskier approach, however, since the growth rate is not guaranteed. This money can be used toward tuition at any accredited school.

Either type of 529 plan has great perks and benefits. All earnings accumulate tax-deferred, and when the money is used, it is taxed at the student's tax rate. Also, the saved money doesn't affect the student's ability to obtain financial aid, as it is not considered part of the student's contribution to the tuition. Specific state plans vary in terms of how they are filed on state tax returns—some states allow deductions for your contributions while others do not tax earnings at all.

There are some restrictions. There is a 10 percent penalty for using the money for anything other than higher education. Also, you cannot switch between the types of plans, although you can contribute to more than one account simultaneously.

State 529 plans are offered in most states. For more information on any of the state plans, call the National Association of State Treasurers at (877) 277-6496.

No matter what plan you decide will work best for you, remember to remain proactive. Keep looking for the better options and always keep your goal in mind: to give your child a good education.

Financial Aid for College

First, you must find out if you qualify for financial aid. You will need to fill out the application forms and send them back to the college(s). From there they are shipped off to agencies that make the ultimate decision on who qualifies and how much they should receive. A needs analysis determines where you stand. This is a calculation made based on your assets and income in conjunction with about 70 percent of the tuition costs of the school (for the rest, you are on your own). Essentially, they will report to the college and the college will then do their own evaluations. Money earmarked for college in your child's name will be weighed more heavily and a higher percentage will be expected to go toward the tuition payments. Therefore, as noted earlier, money in a child's name can work against him or her when applying for financial aid.

Assistance can come from a number of sources, including the federal government (through Pell grants), the state government, the military, or the school itself. It is to your advantage to obtain all of the appropriate forms, fill them out accurately, and submit them on time. Use your tax returns as a guide for filling out the forms.

Scholarships, Grants, and Loans

From an academic scholarship to a cheerleading scholarship, there are a vast number of scholarship opportunities available. Every year billions of dollars are doled out from groups, companies, organizations, and individuals to students to pay part or all of their college tuition. It's hard to believe, but each year there are many more dollars that go unused and unclaimed. The trick is to find out about them, get the forms, and apply.

SallieMae also offers a listing of scholarships. Searching the Internet is yet another way to uncover scholarships you may not have known about. The more obscure the scholarship, the fewer the number of people who apply and the better your chances for being awarded the money. Check out a wide variety of organizations, fraternal groups, associations, and so on to find out who offers scholarship programs. Be careful not to spend money on so called "scholarship finding services," which are often a rip-off.

There are also grants that you can apply for. The Pell grant is a federal grant given to lower-income families; it can provide you with up to $3,000 a year. Other grants (and scholarships) are offered by colleges, based on academic success, athletic ability, or other skills.

Student loans from the federal government still exist, despite cutbacks. Loans are usually based on the interest rate posted on July 1st of each year. The Stafford loan program is a subsidized federal program that is based on need. Repayment begins six months after graduation; students usually have up to ten years to pay it off. An unsubsidized Stafford loan is also available, regardless of need.

Subsidized Stafford loans allow you to borrow up to $2,625 for freshmen, $3,500 for sophomores, and $5,500 for juniors and seniors. During the last two years of college, a student could accumulate a total of $10,500 in loans per year through Stafford. Interest rates will apply.

Perkins loans are provided by the government and administered by the college. They allow you to borrow up to $3,000 per year, and repayment need not start until nine months after graduation. You then have up to ten years to pay it off. These loans are based on need and usually administered by the school.

PLUS loans are not based on financial need. These are personal loans meant for parents and set up through a local bank. They can be given for the entire amount of tuition, but you will need a good credit rating to receive one. The amount of the loan includes housing, transportation, books, and other student needs. The loans are federally backed, and the Federal Student Financial Aid Information Center can provide you with more information (call 800/4-FEDAID). You can also write to the National Education Lending Center, 824 Market Street, Wilmington, DE 19801.

Keep in mind that Perkins loans, Stafford loans, and PLUS loans are all available for undergraduate and graduate school programs.

Questions to Ask When Taking Out a Loan

Inevitably, a loan will be necessary in order to provide for the expense of a college education. Since there are a variety of loans available, it is important to look closely at a few key areas. Some of the terms will be clearly spelled out, but you should always double check the information.

1. What is the interest rate? How is it determined? Is it fixed or varied?
2. How often is interest added to the loan?
3. Are there any stipulations regarding scholarships or other money you may be receiving for college?
4. Can the loan be consolidated with other loans?
5. What fees are there? (Origination fees are common).
6. How long is the grace period?
7. How long do you have to pay back the loan?
8. What repayment plans are available?

Consolidating Education Loans

Since more than one loan source may be needed to finance a college education, you may choose to take advantage of federal consolidation, or consolidating loans from various lenders or programs into one big loan. On the plus side, you'll have just one payment to make, instead of having to spend your time writing out checks to three or four different places. Also, it could take up to thirty years to pay back the loan, and if you consolidate you may get a more "income sensitive" repayment plan, one that could make it easier for you to get a good credit rating.

On the other hand, you may end up with a higher interest rate depending on what is available when you decide to consolidate. Choosing an extended period to pay off any loan can mean that you pay more because you will pay interest for that much longer. And you could lose a deferred status on other loans, meaning you'll have to start paying them off sooner rather than later.

The Payback: A Student's Perspective

Although filling out forms can be a nuisance, the result of receiving college loan money will be thrilling. Unlike a scholarship, this money will need to be paid back upon graduation or leaving school. With any luck at all, college will prepare you for the real world, where a job and steady source of income can make paying back loans more palatable.

College loans may vary in terms of how long you have to pay them back. Generally, payment begins six months after you are out of school and will extend anywhere from ten to fifteen years. There are also several ways in which you will be able to repay your loan. Standard repayment plans usually involve a monthly payment of principle plus interest. Other methods include plans in which you start with reduced payments of interest only and graduate to higher payments including the principle. You end up paying higher total interest, but at least you have lower payments for the first several years out of school when your earning potential is at its lowest.

There are also income sensitive payment plans that vary depending on your income level. Talk with the lender about the types of payback plans. Often students are so excited that their loan applications have been approved that they forget about the repayment process. If you set up this aspect of the loan carefully in advance, you will save yourself headaches later.

A Little Help From the Student

Part of a college education is learning to be part of the real world. One way modern college students can accrue some life lessons is by helping to pay their own way. Summer jobs or part-time jobs during the school year (either on or off campus) can help students pay a lot of their daily expenses. Many colleges waive tuition fees, or at least reduce them, in exchange for work on campus (commonly referred to as work study).

Students can also help themselves by learning how to handle their money wisely. Sharing expenses with roommates, buying used textbooks, and cutting corners are among the many ways students can cut down on expenses. But the key to managing money wisely throughout the college years is to stick to a realistic budget.

A simple budget should list income from part-time money and "gifts" from Mom and Dad on one side of the ledger and anticipated semester expenses in the other. By the second or third semester, students should have the knack of sticking to a budget. Expenses may include tuition payments, board or rent, meals, books, supplies, travel, parking, clothing, laundry, club dues, entertainment, and miscellaneous. The toughest part for the student is trying to keep up with their peers who can afford to spend more. Unfortunately, trying to keep up with the Joneses too often carries well beyond the college years.

chapter thirteen

A Word About Taxes . . . Reduction and Avoidance

For years baseball has been called the great national pastime. But, year round, millions of Americans (over two hundred million) play the real American pastime, that is, trying to figure out how to reduce taxes. There are three primary ways to reduce taxes:

1. Minimize what would be your gross annual income by finding tax-free investments in which to put your money.
2. Take as many itemized deductions as allowable.
3. Earn less money and fall into a lower tax bracket.

The third item is really not a feasible option in terms of jobs and careers. However, if you are on the verge of receiving a large amount of ordinary income and it's December 19th, see if you can defer receiving the money for a few weeks for a particular year, thus avoiding a higher tax bracket.

Tax-Free Investments

There are a number of legal ways to defer or to avoid taxes altogether. Both 401(k) and 403(b) retirement plans, as well as some IRAs, allow you to put away some of your income before paying taxes on it. Depending on the plan, you may have to pay taxes when you withdraw the money. This isn't necessarily a bad thing, since your income level during retirement may be less than it is now. U.S. Treasury bills and U.S. Treasury bonds are places to invest money to avoid state taxes, and municipal bonds are tax-exempt for federal purposes and for state purposes in the state that they are issued.

Compensation that is paid in the form of benefits by your employer for hospitalization, group life insurance, other health plans, or dependent care is not taxable; subject to certain limitations. Furthermore, if you are reimbursed for money spent in direct relation to your employment (e.g., if you are reimbursed for dinner expenses incurred because you had to work late), such payments are not taxable. Also, under flexible spending plans, you can reduce your taxable income by making tax-free salary contributions to plans for reimbursement of expenses for medical or dependent care.

Budgeting to Pay Your Tax Bill

Always set aside a percentage of your income for paying taxes, not unlike an employer withholding a portion of your paycheck for taxes. Put aside a percentage on a monthly basis. If there's a large capital gain, put aside money for the taxes incurred. If you are self-employed, don't forget to set aside money to pay self-employment tax as well as income tax.

Be ready to pay quarterly. However, if you do find yourself unable to pay due to some financial emergency, you can work out a payment plan with the IRS. You will, however, pay interest and possibly penalties.

Some Tax Resources

Some places to seek help, besides tax books in the library, include a couple of leading tax software programs: Turbo Tax Deluxe from Intuit and TaxCut Deluxe from Kiplingers. There are numerous other tax programs available, but many are geared for professional tax preparers and may only add to your confusion.

Besides visiting the IRS Web site (*www.irs.gov*), you can get information from *www.hrblock.com/tax*. The H&R Block site includes new tax laws, ways to itemize, and a calculator for determining your refund.

Conclusion

A lot of ground has been covered in this book. The idea is to present all the information you need to get out and stay out of debt's grasp. With these key points in mind and the willpower to stick with the plan, you should be able to live comfortably without debt. Of course, there is no guarantee of what lies ahead. Emergencies come up, lifestyles change, families grow and these are all factors to consider. Budgeting for these events should make things go a little smoother.

Arm yourself with information, be an informed, cost-conscious, savvy consumer. You work hard for your money and you should work just as hard to ensure that your financial future and that of your family remains secure for many years to come.

Sample Credit Reports

The credit reporting agencies provide three ways to obtain a copy of your credit report. Consumers can request a report by logging on to an agency Web site, writing the agency, or calling the agency directly.

Equifax
P.O. Box 105496
Atlanta GA 30348-5496
800/997-2493
www.equifax.com

Experian
P.O. Box 2104
Allen TX 75013
888/EXPERIAN
www.experian.com

Trans Union
P.O. Box 1000
Chester PA 19022
800/888-4213
www.transunion.com

Following are samples to serve as guides when trying to read and understand a credit report for the first time. For further information on credit reports please refer to *Credit Reports and You*.

SAMPLE 1

YOUR CREDIT REPORT
PO BOX ????
Somewhere, USA 12345
August 1, 2000

Credit Bureau File No. ####
Page 1 of 1
Social Security #########
Date of Birth ######
On file since Mon/Year

Last Name, First Name
Address
City, State, Zip
Phone No.
Former Addresses
123 Maple Drive, Anywhere, USA 54321

Employment Data:
Company Worked for
Date Reported

Your Credit Information

Department Store Card	Account #	Revolving Account
Updated 7/1998	Balance $0	Charge Account
Closed 9/1997	Most owed $500	Individual Account

In prior 1 month from date closed never late

American Bank	Account #	Revolving Account
Updated 1/2000	Balance $2000	Credit Card Limit: $8000
Opened 11/91	Most owed $7594	Pay terms: minimum $42

Status as of 5/2000: Paid or paying as agreed/In prior 48 months never late.

National Bank	Account #	Installment Account
Updated 7/1994	Balance $0	Automobile
Opened 10/1991	Most owed $12,000	Individual Account
Closed 10/94	Pay terms: 60 month $292	

Status of account as of 06/1999: Paid or paying in full

The following companies have received your credit report. Their inquiries remain on your credit report for two years. (Note: Consumer Disclosure inquiries are not viewed by creditors).

Inquiry type	Date	Subscriber Name
Individual	6/22/2000	Consumer Disclosure
Individual	1/02/1999	National Bank
Individual	7/07/1999	Credit Bureau Affiliates
Individual	5/10/1998	American Bank

The following companies obtained information from your consumer report for the purpose of an account review or other business transaction with you. These inquires are not displayed to anyone but you and will never affect any credit decision.

Date	Subscriber Name
01/2000	Nation City Bank
09/1999	National Bank
08/1998	American Bank

If you believe any of the information in your credit report is incorrect, please let us know. For your convenience, an investigation form is included. Please complete it and mail it back to us.

SAMPLE 2

Personal Identification Information
Your Name
Your Current Address
City, State, Zip
Previous Address(es)
Your Previous Address
Last Reported Employment

Social Security Number: #########
Date of Birth: Day Month Year

Your Position and Employer

Public Record Information
Bankruptcy filed on 04/95 in City of Seattle with case or other ID number ########
With Liabilities of $8300, Assets of $50,900, Exempt Amount of $65,000 Type of Personal, Filed Individual, and status Voluntary Ch-7

Collection Agency Account Information

Collection Agency (888) 123-4567

Collection reported 8/99: Assigned 8/95 to Collection Agency. Client City Hospital: Amount $3,000: Unpaid: Balance $3,000: Date of Last Activity 8/95; Individual Account: Account Number ###########

Credit Information

Company Name	Account Number	Whose Account	Date Opened	Last Activity	Type of Account & Status	High Credit	Balance Due	Past	Date Reported
Department Store	######	Individual Past Due	7/80	9/99	Revolving -90 Days	$5,000	$300	$0	10/99
Bank Visa	######	Joint	5/96	11/99	Revolving -Pays As Agreed	$15,000	$1000	$0	12/99
Bank Loan	#####		1/96	1/99	Installment -36 Mos Paid as Agreed	$8500	$0	$0	2/99

Additional Information
Foreclosure reported 5/99 by Company name verified on 5/95

Companies that Requested your Credit File

10/29/99	Department Store Name	08/30/99 Credit Card Company Name - Update
06/23/99	Bank Lender Name	03/04/99 Consumer Disclosure

appendix b

Some Additional Resources

American Association of Individual Investors

The American Association for Individual Investors (AAII) is an independent nonprofit organization. For more than twenty years, it has been helping individuals to invest their own money.

Through various publications, videos, and seminars, the various chapters of AAII help over 175,000 current members by focusing on investing and investment techniques. Their guidance helps both new and seasoned investors and is not limited to those with large sums of money. They are, essentially, a professional association for nonprofessionals.

The membership fee entitles you to their journal, which is published ten times annually and offers how-to articles and information on investing. Perhaps the best feature of the journal is its objectivity; it is not sponsored by investment companies and does not recommend specific investments.

Also included with membership is an annual guide to mutual funds, annual reports, educational materials, and other publications. There are seventy local chapters and several ways to contact AAII; 312/280-0170 (membership services); 800/428-2244 (seminar registration and product information); *www.aaii.com* or *AAII@aol.com*.

American Express Financial Advisors

This well known firm has tons of helpful financial information available on its Web site (*http://finance.americanexpress.com/finance/resources*). There are sections for doing research on companies that you are considering investing in as well as market commentaries from Dow Jones, Forbes, and others. Perhaps the most helpful information can be found in Financial Planning Tools. This is the place to work out your future financial plans for education, equity, investments, education, retirement, estate planning, etc. You can also contact the company directly for information about working one on one with a financial advisor.

National Association of Personal Finance Advisors

The National Association of Personal Finance Advisors (NAPFA) is a membership association dedicated to helping the public receive impartial fee-based financial advice from qualified experts in the field. Members must submit a financial plan, meet education requirements (including strict continuing education requirements), and work on a fee-only basis. NAPFA members should provide comprehensive information on a broad cross section of issues. The only organization of its kind, NAPFA has nearly 600 members throughout the United States. You can contact NAPFA to meet with a financial planner by calling 800/366-2732.

index

FIND MORE ON THIS TOPIC BY VISITING

BusinessTown.com
The Web's big site for growing businesses!

- ☑ **Separate channels on all aspects of starting and running a business**

- ☑ **Lots of info on how to do business online**

- ☑ **1,000+ pages of savvy business advice**

- ☑ **Complete web guide to thousands of useful business sites**

- ☑ **Free e-mail newsletter**

- ☑ **Question and answer forums, and more!**

businesstown.com

visit the

fastread

Home Page at
www.fastread.com

Fastread.com is a new Web site designed to give you the information you need quickly. It covers subjects such as:

- ✦ Investing
- ✦ Personal Finance
- ✦ Getting out of Debt
- ✦ The Internet
- ✦ Building your own Home Page
- ✦ plus more to come!

If you want some tips or facts, and you want them fast, visit **fastread.com**. And remember, your time is money!

 **fastread** FOR THOSE OF US WHO DON'T HAVE ALL DAY!